"Sisterhood not only describes the relationship a woman shares with other women, but also the relationship she has with herself."

— DEBRA J. GAWRYCH

Praise for *The Seven Aspects of Sisterhood: Empowering Women Through Self-Discovery*

ForeWord Magazine Finalist 2001 Book of the Year
Independent Publishers 2002 Book of the Year Award Finalist

"The book is liberally sprinkled with poetry, quotes, exercises, sources for reading, tests, boxed information, and the inclusion of famous (and infamous) names for each aspect variation, i.e. Madonna is a King-Artisan-Storyteller, while Mother Teresa was a Server-Priest-King. It also offers extensive back matter that consists of endnotes, bibliography, and a thorough index.

"The author, speaking in first person, methodically evolves a psychological awareness system for women. Her experience with corporations, nonprofits, and communications gives weight to her sound advice and techniques.

"By changing within, Gawrych says women can empower and change all women as a community. Using this material as a guidebook for workplaces and other groups of people that want to be more productive, improve communication, relieve stress, and simply grow, qualifies as a basic, yet effective self-improving tool."

— *Foreword Magazine*

"It's well done, practical, helpful, and imaginative as well."

— Sally Helgesen,
author of the best-selling *The Female Advantage: Women's Ways of Leadership* and *Thriving in 24/7:*

"Your book is beautiful and full of good ideas!"

—Barbara Bassett, author of *Angela's Word*,
Chicken Soup for a Woman's Soul

"*The Seven Aspects of Sisterhood* was written to help women help themselves to lead better, fuller lives. Gawrych shows women how to analyze their own personalities against the seven archetypal models. Armed with new self-knowledge, one is ready to better understand and react to the many trials that daily life has in store. Very highly recommended reading for women of all ages, backgrounds, and circumstances."

— *Midwest Book Review*

"In *The Seven Aspects of Sisterhood: Empowering Women through Self-Discovery*, Debbie Gawrych has written a powerful book of depth, clarity, and heart. Her premises are clear, and her research is impeccable. She opens up a wider world of understanding, while also offering practical tips and action steps to foster personal growth and mastery."

— Robert "Dusty" Staub,
author of *The Heart of Leadership* and *The 7 Acts of Courage*

"An amazing book. One I couldn't put down. I took it on a three day yoga retreat and gave it to other flight attendants to read on our regular flight to Tokyo. They loved it!"

— Ann Hardee, Director of Fitness Instructors,
Pyramids Wellness Centers

"*The Seven Aspects of Sisterhood* allows the reader to identify their personality traits and grow. The book instructively empowers individual understanding of the dynamics of one's unique combination of traits. I highly recommend this book. It is in constant demand in our library."

"For the Pioneer Women of the *New* Century. I've found the perfect map. It is simple to understand and will take us far. I love your book."

— Ann Westergaard, Shaklee

"*The Seven Aspects of Sisterhood* is a perceptive look into how women relate to one another, says author Debra. J. Gawrych. It points women in the direction of understanding themselves in order to be more effective working with other women—on the job, in a family, or in an organization."

— *Rapid River Digest*

"I very much want to carry this book in the ArisingArts catalog! Because Gawrych promotes acceptance and understanding, and does this sort of thing extraordinarily well."

— SophiArising Publications

"...a pleasantly concise self-help book that encourages women to gain control of their feelings and motives in order to rise above stress. Such solid advice as 'Choice is about taking a breath and realizing the possibilities in a situation instead of feelings hopeless' is dispensed cleanly, unclouded by excessive New Age babble."

— *Mountain Express*, Asheville, NC

"...excellent new self-help book."

— *Expansion*

"I loved *The Seven Aspects of Sisterhood: Empowering Women Through Self-Discovery*. It encourages all women to find their true passion and to walk the heroine's journey, while still appreciating the world around them. It is a true reminder that we are all sisters, and that we should always appreciate the many gifts that we individually have to offer this world."

— Tracey Burchette-Simmons, Senior Partner,
Staub Leadership Consultants

"I am impressed with the research she has done for this and the way she has organized her theory. It has such an attractive cover that it will draw the eye when it is displayed in all the big bookstores and libraries."

— Janet Hill

"Your achievement is stunning, marvelous, and amazing. Congratulations on your new book!"

— Carol Kormelink

"What a beautiful book!"

— Reverend Melissa Bowers, author of "Praise to the Women on My Journey," from *Chicken Soup for a Woman's Soul*

"In her maiden book, Debra J. Gawrych explores seven personality types, the goals and obstacles associated with each, and the ways in which owners of each type can learn to gain a vision of their inner selves and the other types they interact with day-to-day."

— *Today's American Woman*

"I really like your book. I am trying, at this stage of my life—65, to rethink things and get myself back in order."

— Nancy Easter

the 7 Aspects of Sisterhood

Empowering Women Through Self-Discovery

the 7 Aspects of Sisterhood

Empowering Women
Through Self-Discovery

Debra J. Gawrych

common boundaries
CONSULTING &
COMMUNICATIONS

Greensboro, North Carolina

Published by Common Boundaries
P.O. Box 39445
Greensboro, NC 27438
336-288-8554
www.commonboundaries.com

ISBN 0-9710646-0-1
Library of Congress Control Number: 2001089251

Printed in the United States of America
First Edition

Design & Editorial Services by The Roberts Group
Cover Design by Gemini Group

Permission to reprint copyrighted material: see page 247.

A portion of the proceeds from the sale of this book go to charities including: Expedition Inspiration, founded by Laura Evans to raise funds for breast cancer research and promote self-esteem for breast cancer survivors, and to the Women's World Bank, an international not-for-profit institution chartered to provide economic development by lending small loans directly to women living at the poverty level in thirty-seven countries. These women are empowered and encouraged to be entrepreneurs and to become part of the solution to their problems.

My Neighbour

I am glad you made my neighbour different from me;
A different coloured skin, a different shaped face;
A different response to you.
I need my neighbour to teach me about you:
She knows all the things I don't know.

MONICA FURLONG
*Laughter, Silence and Shouting:
An Anthology of Women's Prayers*

CONTENTS

Together We Seek the Way

Loving God
Together we seek the way,
Helping, watching, learning, leading,
Each step forging new links,
Each dialogue opening further
The channels of peace and understanding.
We stand poised on the brink of greatness,
Drawn by the Spirit into new realms of hope and trust.
The barriers of past centuries
Are slowly crumbling.
We pray that the skeletons of division and discord
Will be laid to rest,
And that the people of God will be fully mobilized.
For these and all your mercies,
We thank and praise you, O God.

ST. HILDA COMMUNITY
Laughter, Silence and Shouting:
An Anthology of Women's Prayers

PREFACE

Being a woman in this day and time is special. It means pulling together god-given talents to help change our world for the better. Along with freedom, today's women have an unprecedented amount of responsibility. Thirty years after the second wave of the feminist revolution, women reap the benefits in terms of freedom of expression, mobility, and choice. At the same time, women have crawled out from under stereotypes of the feminine nature, but have kept the feminine qualities.

This means that it is acceptable for women to be mysterious, moody, flexible, nurturing, and changing. These facets of women are accepted as an integral part of woman's nature instead of looked upon as a curse or a defect that needs to be cut out of existence. The biggest indication of this change is that even in our patriarchal society, men are beginning to embrace these qualities in themselves. Women have the freedom, the tools, and the qualities to lend in the process of integrating what is good from the masculine and feminine.

The sisterhood works under the principles of community or group dynamics. When it is operating in harmony—towards a common goal—extraordinary things are accomplished. When it is operating under stress, the group falls into disarray and little is accomplished. Therefore, it is beneficial to all women to understand the part they play, perform to the best of their ability, and understand the tremendous gift they have to offer the group (sisterhood) at large.

The community of women is composed of millions of women who come from various cultures and who, although alike by virtue of their sex, possess different personalities, needs, and beliefs. Whether they are conscious of it or not, they form the "glass window" of the sisterhood. When they come together in tension and strife, the window clouds over, may have nicks in it, and is difficult to see through. When anger mounts and jealousy seeps in, the window may crack and even shatter, rendering it useless—and the sisterhood is in pieces. When women work together and empower each other, the window is clear and strong and able to transmit light at the optimal level.

Yet the sisterhood is more than a community of women. It is also the relationship that a woman has with herself. It is about becoming authentic and learning to listen to the different voices that make up a woman's own internal guidance system. Each woman is made up of many parts and is a complex being. Each woman is a hologram of the larger community of women and, in order to find her place, she must seek to understand herself first. This hologram is more than just a bundle of varied emotions; it is a picture of our true identity. Therefore, each woman is a sisterhood unto herself.

Looking inward helps to connect us with the creative energy available to us from archetypal dimensions. These patterns or archetypes are universally recognized themes or images that provide a common language for human experience and are derived from what Carl Jung called the *collective unconscious*.

This book helps name and identify different aspects or personalities in women. In doing so, the hope is that once a woman has gained better understanding of herself, it will translate into a better understanding of other people. In other words, "if I'm comfortable with who I am, I'll be more willing to allow you the space to be who you are."

The Seven Aspects Personality Model is based on a system that describes personality in terms of various elements that overlay our true essence or soul. The fundamental principle of the system is that we have a choice between acting from the positive or negative parts of our personality. Choosing to act from the positive may counterbalance the tension created when we act out of the negative part.

What we show to the world as personality and the search for our true self becomes a balancing act. As we observe the work that goes into this act of balance, we are able to identify with the struggles of everyone else who is doing the same. This recognition leads to identification with the common denominator we all face—human nature—and enables us to see the personality and actions of others with a nonjudgmental point of view.

The underlying principles of this model may be seen in Carl Jung's type psychology and the works of Fritjof Capra, Abraham Maslow, Eric Erickson, Stanislov Grof, Louise Hay, Chris Griscom, and Joseph Campbell, as well as José Stevens, Simon Warwick-Smith, and Emily Baumbach. The premise of the Seven Aspects Model is acceptance of self and others, which is the key element to reaching the goal of unconditional love.

Today's women are facing a transition; there is a global change in the air. The wind is shifting towards a new paradigm of what it means to be a woman. There is a groundswell of support to view both men and women as not only our physical bodies, but as also being something more. This something more encompasses our emotions, our hopes and dreams, our inner voice and energy, and is the essence of who we truly are. The awareness that comes with this recognition is our connection to the collective unconscious. When we listen to this inner awareness, it becomes our unique road map towards wholeness that can steer us through the chaos of daily life.

This book is meant to be a tool to help you on your own journey of self-discovery. It is not a definitive psychological or spiritual work. It is an invitation to continue your journey in a more conscious manner. Use the material as an inner-directed guidebook. Read the book at your pace, using the concepts as steppingstones to help you reach your destination. The path can start anywhere, but must eventually lead inside for greater awareness. With a little help from other women, their wit, and their wisdom, we sisters can empower each other to take one step at a time towards a greater vision of what we can be.

ACKNOWLEDGMENTS

I would like to gratefully acknowledge the many people who have believed in me and helped me along the way to make this book a reality. To the teachers in my life who inspired me and taught me the basic principles upon which this book is founded: Norma Robinson and Kay Grant, two high school teachers who asked me to "go make waves and touch people's hearts"; Nancy Willis, a guiding light who helped me through key turning points in my life; and Chris Mamman, who now lives in Nigeria, and was a tennis pro who taught me so much more than tennis. From all of my teachers, I have learned to be resilient and believe in myself. Daily, I see the infinite wisdom and synchronicity of the universe that brought us together. Thank you.

Friends and family: thank you to Doug, my benevolent (King) husband, for his acceptance and tolerance of years of dedication to my goals; my children: Christopher (Warrior), Audrey (Artisan), and Gavin (Priest), who have taught me many lessons, some of which I have included in this book; my mother, Opalee Jacquot, for edit work and for giving me her unconditional love; my father Earl, for being the calm in the center of the Jacquot sisterhood; my brother Ken and his wife, Beth, for art and marketing support.

I also wish to express my gratitude to: Cameron Cooke, for his effervescent networking support and guidance in teaching me about community and finding one's way in the world; Dusty and Tina Staub, for lending ideas and support, being great friends, and introducing me to Patricia Wisdom; Lori Wainright, for listening, proofing, and prodding me to dig deeper; Kathy Morton, for being a friend and lending support not only for the book, but for other parts of my life as well; Linda Wagstaff, Allison MacMillian, Lisa Adornetto, Sarah Williams, and the countless people who took the personality test; Wayne Gerber and Brock Holden, for giving critiques; Abby Donnelly, for reviewing several chapters; Tracey Simmons, for love, encouragement, and support; the staff at Staub Leadership Consultants, who has supported my dream; Lily Kelly-Radford, who encouraged me to live my dream; Michael Tomlinson, whom I consider a friend through his writing and music, and who is encouraging others to live respectfully with other people; and Sandra Redding, who encouraged me to write.

To Emily Baumbach, a wonderful teacher and friend who dedicated her personal time to provide data and moral support, I give a heartfelt thanks. Whether over the phone, via e-mail, or in person, you gave me great information and unconditional support. Namaste. To José Stevens and Simon Warwick-Smith, the body of your work has been extensive. Thank you so much for your writing and for the permission to expand on your material.

Other thanks go to: Cindy Tierney, my faithful assistant and associate editor who keeps me organized; and Laura Goodman, who with her diligence and eagle eye for detail was the perfect person to proof the manuscript. Also to: Barbara Linnville, Cindy Valliere, and Betsy Willard, facilitators who really know how to connect. To Marian Stewart and Grant Thompson, of the Gemini Group, thank you for your artistic vision and creations. You helped bring to life what I could only imagine.

To Sherry Roberts, of The Roberts Group, my tireless and persevering editor and friend, words truly cannot describe the value-added service you provided. You didn't flinch when I added thirty pages after editing and calmly listened to my ideas. Your literary skill greatly enhanced my wording and presentation of the material. I would not have wanted to do this with anyone else. It was synchronicity again.

To the hundreds of people along the way who listened patiently as I developed my ideas, to the writers of the many books that helped give substance to my thoughts, and to all of the women and men who helped me in this journey—thank you, this book is for you.

The Truth of the Sisterhood

We start as a grain of sand.
  rolling and turning,
  tumbling and jumbling,
  nudged along by the currents of life
  battered about by the waves of emotion.
Along the way we run into other grains
  just like us and
  perhaps a little different:

A different shape
A different texture
A different color.

We bump into some grains
  and rejoice in the meeting
It feels good to have contact,
  as if we met an old friend.
We share much in common.
It feels right.
We want to stay together but,
  are pulled by the current to a new place,
  where we run into more grains of sand.

Some are rough and irritate like sandpaper.
Others seem distant and dull
  and want to be left alone.
Still others are mean and
  band with other grains to smother us.

We feel frightened and try to roll away,
  but the current is too strong.
It pulls us back to,
  the grains we don't like.
We search for a friendly face.
We yearn for the grains we met before,
  the ones with whom we feel most comfortable.
We feel stuck and frustrated
  and remain there until
  we begin to see the possibilities.

We begin to like where we are
  even without our comforts
We find that given time
  the dull and distant grains
  come to us and are willing to be friends
We find that the grains that feel like sandpaper
  can be softened by rubbing against them.
We wonder if there are other possibilities
  for the grains of sand that have tried
  to smother us.

We observe them
 as they bustle and jumble together
  and feel the heat they create.
At first it agitates and irritates,
  but later on we observe that given enough time
  the heat serves to melt each grain ever so slightly
  so that eventually they begin to look alike.

The more time they spend together,
  the more heat they generate.
And they blend together so much,
  that it becomes difficult to tell
  where one grain begins and another ends.

And thus we observe the formation
  of the sisterhood.
From tiny individual grains of sand,
  through friendship and comfort
  through irritation and adversity,
  we come together to
  create something bigger than ourselves,
  bigger than our own grain of sand.
We are fused together through heat
  to create glass.
And from glass we form a window
  from which the truth of our existence
  can clearly shine through.

DEBRA J. GAWRYCH
June 25, 2000

CHAPTER ONE

THE SEVEN ASPECTS
OF SISTERHOOD

Women are wonderfully complex people. They are inherently different, both physically and emotionally from men. Women can bear children, have different hormones, and are subject to different emotional responses. A woman experiences stages, which are unique to her, throughout her life. Contained within her being is a complex mix of characteristics, and she expresses this uniqueness to the outer world as her aspects. This is what she shares with the greater community of women. Sisterhood not only describes the relationship a woman shares with other women, but also the relationship she has with herself.

Each woman is unique. She has her own style, her own grace or lack thereof. She comes from different cultures, different families. She may be rich or poor, nurturing or tough. She may be mathematically inclined or unable to balance her checkbook. She may be athletic or artistic. The challenge for a woman is to believe in her own self-worth and to understand that honoring her uniqueness helps give her authenticity and elevates her action to the highest level of integrity. In effect, e more she understands and accepts the different aspects of herself, the more whole she becomes.

Women tend to bond together. This starts as early as elementary school with the cliques of girls who include and exclude other girls based on whether or not they have enough in common to be "in." This process of bonding together and pulling away when disagreements arise persists throughout a woman's lifetime.

It is a process of learning to pay attention and to let go. It is also a process of becoming clearer about our motives and intent. We can be more objective about disagreements when we ask ourselves if our actions are in alignment with out principles. As M.J. Ryan writes in *The Fabric of the Future*, "At the confluence of the two millennia, one of the most challenging insecurities to be overcome is that felt by people in relation to themselves—the question: Who am I?"[1]

Who we are and who we show to the world can be different and is the personality mix we carry with us. I refer to this mix as our *aspects*. In the case of two women, one may be outgoing and the other shy. It doesn't mean that the outgoing woman can't be quiet or that the shy woman can't assert herself. It means that different aspects of their personality are dominant.

These aspects guide the expression of our personalities throughout our life and are the driving force behind how we react with our environment and other people. One aspect is not better than another. For example, it is no better to possess a high degree of the "King" aspect and live a powerful life as the leader of an organization or CEO of a corporation, than it is to be a behind-the-scenes "Server" or an "Artisan" who drifts from job to job. What is more important is the integrity of each woman and how closely she is living her life to her core principles and values.

The Seven Aspects are expressed to different degrees in what we show to the world as our personalities and are as follows:

Warrior   King
Priest   Server
Artisan   Storyteller
Scholar

Some of these aspects or roles are obvious; some may be more difficult to see. In this book, I have provided a Self-Identification Test to help you determine your aspects. This book also contains a detailed explanation of each aspect, which can be used as a tool to better understand yourself and to improve your relationship with other women. It is important to understand as much as you can about yourself and be at peace with yourself in order to truly be okay with other people, especially other women.

Determining your own aspects and tendencies will increase your understanding about why we are different and how we can work together to bring out the best in each other. When we stop judging each other, we give each other the space to express who we truly are. The positive feelings flow upward in a never-ending spiral of support, instead of moving downward into a pit of judgment. This supportive space is essential for the development of self-esteem. And when self-esteem is supported, communication and relationships improve. The result is women living and working together in harmony, a sisterhood. It is possible.

The Relationship of the Seven Aspects

It is easier to understand the Seven Aspects if you think of them as personality types. Each aspect symbolizes characteristics present in everyone's personality, yet the model encourages us to look at which aspect is the most predominate. This helps us understand the tendencies and patterns each person demonstrates in his or her interactions with other people. Six of the aspects act as companions to each other; the seventh, Scholar, occupies a neutral role and is a companion to all of the aspects. (See figure 1.1.)

> ➤ The two companion roles of **Warrior** and **King** are action roles. Both are dynamic people who demonstrate a lot of activity in their lives, activity that they do or that they direct others to do.

> ➤ **Priest** and **Server** (Inspiration) also are companion roles and are focused on inspiring others to do their best.

FIGURE 1.1

The Relationship of the Seven Aspects

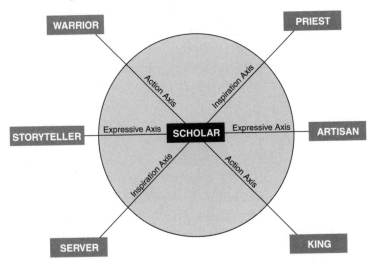

> ➤ The two companion roles of **Artisan** and **Storyteller** (Expressive) are gifted with communicating to others. Storytellers communicate with words, and Artisans communicate with things.

> ➤ The last role, **Scholar** (Neutral), is concerned with the study and interpretation of ideas. A Scholar records information and helps the other aspects incorporate what she has learned into everyday experiences. Scholars mediate between aspects and are helpful to have on committees and teams.

The Scholar is a neutral aspect and can get along with any of the aspects. A Scholar tends to be less prone to emotional outburst. This aspect is the natural voice of reason.

To get a better handle on the seven aspects, we can look at how they relate to each other. (See figure 1.2.) Some aspects are leaders, and some are implementers by nature. Leaders have the quality of focusing outward or taking a broad perspective, while implementers pursue a more specific focus.

FIGURE 1.2

The Relationship of One Aspect to Another

	Implementer		Leader
Role	**Specific Focus**	**Neutral**	**Broad Focus**
Action	Warrior		King
Inspiration	Server		Priest
Expression	Artisan		Storyteller
Assimilation		Scholar	

The broad-focused or leader aspects of King, Priest, and Storyteller are more broad-minded and more likely to require attention and being in the spotlight. They provide leadership by their ability to deal with large groups of people, and prefer to have the attention focused on them and what they are doing. In doing so, they tend to stand out more than the other aspects.

The implementer aspects—Warrior, Server, and Artisan—are more specifically focused. As long as they complete their chosen tasks, they are content without the spotlight. They have a more "down-to-earth" approach and illustrate the premise that not everyone can be the leader. There are more implementers (Warriors, Artisans, and Servers) than there are leaders (Kings, Priests, and Storytellers).

People who possess the specific-focused aspects are more numerous in the population as they thrive on one-to-one interactions. They are focused on immediate tasks. There are fewer people of the broad-focused aspects since only a few are needed to deal with the masses. They love to be in the limelight and bask in the attention of dealing with large groups of people.

This is not to imply that the specific-focused aspects are any less important than the broad-focused aspects. Each aspect or role has a special purpose and is essential in order for the other aspects to fulfill their purposes. *All aspects are equally important!* This is important to remember if we want to improve communications and relations with each other.

Where would a leader (**King**) be without people to lead? Where would mankind be without the beauty created by the **Artisans**? Without the people who give unselfishly of themselves (**Servers**)? Without the people who have the courage to stand up for what is right (**Warriors**)? Without people who remind us of the sacredness of life (**Priests**)? Without the cut-ups and comics (**Storytellers**)? Without the mediators who are the voice of reason in a time of conflict (**Scholars**)?

The mix of the percentages of the aspects in the population varies. As people are born and pass away, it changes. It also varies from country to country due to cultural influences. Figure 1.3 provides the most recent estimate of the mix for women within the United States. Although references may be made for the general population, it is more accurate to assess on a specific basis, such as for a given country or for a given population at a certain period of time.

Recently, there has been a significant shift from the dominant Primary Aspect of women Warriors to women Artisans. There is also a growing percentage of Scholars and Priests for the Primary Aspect. This can be seen, according to author Emily Baumbach, with the growing number of women involved in new technologies and inventions in the areas of science, business, and media, especially the Internet.

FIGURE 1.3

Percentages of the Aspects in the Population

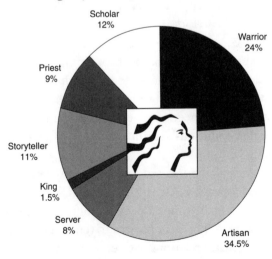

Source: These percentages are approximations provided by Emily Baumbach, author of *Celebrities: The Complete Michael Database, Personality Profiles for Over 1,000 Famous People.* She assesses personality profiles using a complementary model and are current for May 2001.

Self-Identification Assessment

Look over the following sentences. As you read them, visualize interacting with others. You may see a bit of yourself in all of the sentences; still you need to decide the degree to which the sentence is true. In considering your answer, use your first instinct. Do not overanalyze and try to predetermine the outcome. Your response needs to be the **one** that feels the most like who you really are; **not whom others think you are or what you'd like to be.** Mark each sentence in the line provided as to whether it is: Not True (1), Somewhat True (2), Half True (3), Mostly True (4), or True (5).

After each section, subtotal your answer. At the end of the test, you will use the top three highest scores to determine your aspects. Use the accompanying answer key and scoring blocks to record your Primary, Secondary, and Tertiary (Third) Aspects. These will be explained in the information following the test. The three answers comprise the "triad" of your self, your own unique sisterhood.

After determining your aspects, read the detailed explanations that follow. As you read the explanations, consider women in your life with whom you have conflicts and those with whom you feel comfortable. What are their aspects? Then read the explanations of their aspects for clues about how to improve your interactions with them.

> **Self-Identification Assessment Scoring**
>
> 1 — Not True
> 2 — Somewhat True
> 3 — Half True
> 4 — Mostly True
> 5 — True

Section I

1. I love to take care of people and see to it that they are comfortable.   3

2. I'd rather work behind the scenes making sure that everything is under control.   5

3. Serving others directly is what inspires me the most in life.   3

4. I have difficulty confronting people and can be passive-aggressive.   2

Self-Identification Assessment

5. I feel best when I put others' needs before my own. _2_

6. I am satisfied not being the leader. _3_

Subtotal _18_

Section II

7. I feel compassion for people in pain and seek to heal them physically, emotionally, and spiritually. _2_

8. I often feel a strong urge to tell people what I think is best for them. _2_

9. I have a deep sense of mission about my life. _2_

10. Sometimes I am zealous in pursuing what I perceive to be the higher good. _2_

11. I am charismatic and inspire others with my vision. _2_

12. Inside I feel like a finely tuned instrument. _1_

Subtotal _11_

Section III

13. If I can't express my creativity, I feel blocked and frustrated. _1_

14. I love to create atmosphere, moods, and situations. _1_

15. Often I feel so creative, I don't know what to do first. _1_

16. Life is my canvas. I want to express myself in a unique way. _1_

17. I need time to daydream. _2_

18. I am quick to grasp ideas and am a pioneer. _1_

Subtotal _7_

Section IV

19. I like to relate to people by telling stories. _2_

20. If it's not fun, I usually don't want to do it. _2_

21. I like the attention of a group or crowd, and entertaining them is a skill of mine. _1_

22. I'm not opposed to "bending the truth" for the right cause. _2_

Self-Identification Assessment

23. I am persuasive and can lead and inspire others to my viewpoint.   *1*

24. I possess wisdom and enjoy teaching by sharing stories with others.   *1*

Subtotal   *9*

Section V

25. I like to get things organized.   *5*

26. I am a doer and most importantly want results.   *4*

27. It's the principle of the thing that counts.   *4*

28. If I take on a project, I will complete it to the best of my abilities.   *4*

29. I have a great deal of energy and enjoy using it to accomplish something I value.   *2*

30. I am honest to a fault and can sometimes be blunt.   *2*

Subtotal   *21*

Section VI

31. If I do a task, I do it with excellence.   *2*

32. I am able to communicate the big picture.   *2*

33. I would rather delegate than do the work.   *2*

34. I feel responsible for the welfare of others.   *2*

35. I want to be in a position of authority.   *2*

36. Groups of people look up to me.   *2*

Subtotal   *12*

Section VII

37. I am innately curious and like to study things.   *1*

38. I learn from the past to make decisions about the future.   *2*

39. I can be neutral and an effective mediator.   *3*

40. I pursue knowledge avidly and record it all.   *1*

Self-Identification Assessment

41. I love to read and research.   _1_

42. I wait to make decisions until I have weighed all the facts.   _2_

Subtotal   _10_

Compute the subtotals for each section and find your three highest numbers. Note the section numbers of your three highest subtotals. Find their corresponding aspects using the answer key below.

Answer Key:

Section I	Server
Section II	Priest
Section III	Artisan
Section IV	Storyteller
Section V	Warrior
Section VI	King
Section VII	Scholar

14

12

21

Make a note of your aspects:

Primary Aspect (highest total) _____ *V*
This is your most prominent personality type.

Second Aspect (second highest total) _____ *1 Server*
This aspect complements the Primary Aspect and is a way of rounding out or adding complexity to your personality.

Third Aspect (third highest total) _____ *12 Storyteller*
This aspect is your link to the rest of the world. It helps you relate to other aspects in yourself and others.

After you take the assessment: Read about your aspects and how they relate to each other in the next section. This information also will be useful as you become aware of the aspects of other women.

An In-Depth Look at Each Aspect

Warrior

A Warrior woman is a catalyst for change. She is someone who works hard to achieve a goal and encourages others to do so. She can show masculine attributes and, at the same time, be feminine. She is someone who has the courage to do what has traditionally been considered within a man's domain and complete any task she sets her mind to do. She is not afraid of expressing both her masculine and feminine sides (see figure 1.6). She is a pioneer spirit—creative, attentive, and courageous.

She is also curious and impulsive. She may react before she thinks; in other words, she "shoots from the hip." She is a hard worker and may be intolerant of others who don't possess the same work ethic. Although she flourishes under the direction of a King, she also may find herself in leadership roles. In such cases, she will be most content when the leadership roles are "hands on." Warrior women do not like to be the "up-front person." In spite of their tremendous ability to organize, they prefer to have a King as the person to assume the ultimate responsibility.

A Warrior is quick—quick to grasp ideas, to react, to change direction, and also quick to make mistakes. She is a good student and can make a good teacher. When not checked, her impulsive tendencies could be likened to those of being "a bull in a china shop."

She feels empowered when coming from her most self-actualized state: when she is the integration of both feminine and masculine characteristics.

FIGURE 1.6

Masculine and Feminine Traits

Feminine	Masculine
creative	analytical
soft	hard
yin	yang
curve	linear
yield	drive
give	push
nurture	instruct
chaos	order
clutter	organize
listen	speak
follow	lead
circumlocutious	straightforward
restrained	energetic
rest	active
compassionate	authoritative
fluid	solid
peaceful	dynamic

Many women today possess the Warrior aspect. These women approach life through their five senses. They tend to be physical and like to be at the center of things. They like to earn what they have. The satisfaction is in the striving. They can only enjoy what they achieve when they feel they have truly earned it.

Warriors can be prone to tunnel vision and be so focused on the goal that they lose sight of people and things around them. A mature woman with strong Warrior aspects will be more nurturing than an immature one. This has nothing to do with age, but with the maturity of the personality and the soul. Warriors tend to be their own worst critics, and the degree to which they are tough on others illustrates the degree they are tough on themselves.

How Warriors Relate to Others

Warriors are the worker bees of society and are one of the most numerous aspects of women today. Author Emily Baumbach estimates that most of the population of the United States is comprised of Warriors, 24 percent, and Artisans, 34.5 percent (both men and women). Warriors love planning and control and being organized. They are commonly found in parent-teacher organizations, leading volunteer efforts in church or community, as stay-at-home moms who coordinate family activities, and in business. Whenever possible, Warrior women may be found creating and operating large organized social bureaucracies such as the educational system, healthcare, and government.

These women have a sense of what is right and wrong and will fight for their beliefs. They can be combative and must be careful to check their argumentative impulses if they want to get along with others. In a very real sense, they are "warriors." They are the first to rush into "battle," be it an argument at home or in the courtroom. Perhaps that is because we typically associate women with drive and assertiveness as athletes, business leaders, or "a woman with balls." We find woman Warrior icons in the media: "Thelma and Louise," "Mulan," "La Femme Nikita," Hillary Clinton, and "GI Jane." These are women who affect change, women who transform.

Warrior women typically make good parents because their families run like clockwork. Discipline is quick and just. Their children know exactly what is expected of them and know the consequences if they misbehave.

They are honest to a fault and can be blunt if not careful. They have an inherent dislike for "sleazy personalities" that bend the truth or present it in creative ways. Women warriors teach their children about the aspects of marketing and to be wary of the "strong sell."

They love drama and when bored actually create situations to entertain themselves. They may cause an argument just to keep busy. Women Warriors are often athletes and tend to have strong bodies. They have a tendency to lead more adventurous or active lifestyles.

Positive Characteristics of Warriors [2]

Warriors are productive, structured, organized, assertive, driven, confronting, focused, Robin Hood-like, truthful, resourceful, determined, family-oriented, protective, maternal, defending, skilled, grounded, practical, proud, and principled. They value the intellectual.

They are good at setting up structures that care for other people: in schools, churches, hospitals, and the community. They are the visible society builders and provide the foundation of civilization so that the Artisans can provide culture.

Negative Characteristics of Warriors

Warriors can be bullying, narrow-minded, intimidating, pushy, emotionally withheld, overwrought, stressed, subjective, hot-tempered, overbearing, blunt, tactless, looking for struggle or conflict, argumentative, abrasive, unforgiving, mistrustful, brutal, suspicious, devious, and coercive.

If not careful, Warriors can resort to intimidation to get their way. Sometimes because of their intense focus, they may not understand why other people are frightened of them. They may not see that they are creating the very situation they seek to avoid.

Famous Warriors[3]

Julie Andrews, Attila the Hun, Lauren Bacall, Ellen Barkin, Shirley Temple Black, Marcia Clark, Hillary Clinton, Glenn Close, Joan Crawford, Bette Davis, Don Juan, Clint Eastwood, Chris Evert, Geraldine Ferraro, Jane Fonda, Richard Gere, Indira Ghandi, Ruth Bader Ginsburg, John Grisham, Christie Hefner, Ernest Hemingway, Don Henley, Angelica Houston, Jackie Joyner-Kersee, Billie Jean King, Nelson Mandela, Golda Meir, Demi Moore, Martina Navratilova, Paul Newman, Princess Anne, Robert Redford, Janet Reno, Joan Rivers, Nicole Brown Simpson, Gertrude Stein, Martha Stewart, Sharon Stone.

King

The King aspect is rarely found. It is estimated that less than 2 percent (approximately 1.5 percent) of the *total* population (including men) are Kings at any point in time.[4] Why? Not everyone can be a leader. Kings by nature lead. Their focus is broad-minded. They act "royally," meaning they have the ability and charisma to give the orders that others will gladly carry out. In fact, some people may even volunteer to serve for Kings before being asked. It can be said that a little King goes a long way, and of course, too many Kings wouldn't do at all.

Because the world has been male-dominated for the past 2,000–3,000 years, few women have been able to ascend to positions of power that would utilize the Primary Aspect of the King. Therefore, the majority of Kings in our recent history have been men. These have been the presidents, CEOs, and leaders of the past and present times.

A friend of mine asked a pointed question about the use of "King" as a personality archetype as opposed to "Queen." My response was that it was a good point, but that right or wrong, "Queen" does not connote mental imagery of supremacy, as does the word "King." A King can be a woman or a man. The King aspect is about power and vision. It is about strategic guidance, being the ultimate leader as opposed to one who carries out the work. The image of visionary power has been translated into masculine form in our culture. So to understand the concept of "King," we must, for now, use the same language.

Women who possessed the innate aspects of King found creative ways to fulfill their needs in the past. Rose Kennedy is such an example. As the matriarch of the Kennedy clan, she was looked to by all of the family members for strength and leadership and is a good illustration of the King aspect. In fact, one of the reasons the Kennedy family has commanded such attention is the preponderance of Kings among them. Rose Kennedy, John F. Kennedy, and Jacqueline Kennedy Onassis were all considered Kings. It is unusual to find even one King in a family, so to have three is extremely powerful.

Women Kings of the past may have felt thwarted and constrained by the limits society placed on them. Most likely these women were found leading and directing their families in a matriarchal role. Other roles could have been as diverse as choir director or the town beautician, who would be the center of information and who could direct others with advice in a decidedly nonthreatening way. Some of these women ascended to leadership positions in more traditionally accepted roles, in teaching, nursing, or volunteer efforts. Others were able to transcend limitations. Wives of some leaders have been Kings (Raisa Gorbachev, Elizabeth Dole) as well as some women who have been the leaders of their own country, such as India's Indira Ghandi.

Many women were allowed positions of leadership and power only to the extent that it did not threaten their male counterparts or any sense of male authority. These women had to be resourceful to survive. They needed to quickly assess what was going on around them and adapt to the constraints placed on them. These women surely felt frustration. And out of this frustration, they discovered creative ways to fulfill their destinies.

Kings are best at leading and do so with dignity, almost always with the well-being of the people they lead in mind. A King wants everyone to win. They almost have a prophetic sense of how things will unfold; therefore, they are excellent strategic planners and "think-tankers."

How Kings Relate to Others

Kings love recognition and to be in positions of authority. As such, a King may often be heard to say, "I want this task completed and on my desk by such and such time." They make excellent managers, politicians, presidents, and CEOs. A King has a regal bearing. Some may feel they are distant or aloof, but this is part of their "kingly" nature. In order to lead, they must be able to create distance from those they seek to lead.

They have an innate ability to bring people together. They inspire others and can "rally the troops" for a good cause. Responsibility is a key word for them. They feel an acute sense of responsibility for the people they draw to them and for the outcome of the task at hand.

Mastery is another key word. They enjoy being at the head of wherever they are: their company, church, community, or family. They may exhibit "kingly" qualities within the family unit and be concerned with "launching" each family member into his or her respectful path in life.

They are usually the first or last born: an ideal elder brother or a youngest child who becomes the confidant of both parents and siblings.

A King who is immature may be selfish in her visions, which may consist more of personal power than positive outcomes for the community at large. More mature Kings are compassionate and could also be found in roles such as on the board of a volunteer group or directing volunteer efforts, for example, a Habitat for Humanity project.

Kings get along well with most roles, but have an affinity for Servers. Servers get their satisfaction "serving" others, and Kings get their satisfaction leading others or being served. Warriors, Artisans, and Scholars are also good aspects for a King. These aspects are driven externally to express and are giving. Warriors act as the catalysts who lead the battle charge, while Artisans make the world a more pleasant place in which to live, and Scholars provide the research for the King to make informed choices about how to lead. Aspects that tend to clash with the King aspect are those of Priest and Storyteller. These two both require recognition and can battle the King for the limelight.

The King aspect appears more frequently in countries such as the United States, Japan, and Germany. They appear infrequently in India and the more densely populated Third World countries, which because of cultural differences, don't encourage personal achievement as much as the U.S.[5] The United States and other developed countries tend to value uniqueness and competitiveness. This being the case, there are more chances for a King to ascend to power in those countries. This may change as Third World countries develop and may already be changing in China as it gains prominence in economic and political power in the world.

Positive Characteristics of Kings

Kings imprint the goal of striving for excellence on those around them. They are natural leaders, gentle, magnanimous, charismatic, strategists, visionaries, self-assured, stable, regal, well-rounded, commanding, informed, good at delegating, good with money, and quiet and more gentle than Warriors. They get along well with others and inspire loyalty, commitment, and devotion.

Negative Characteristics of Kings

Kings can be demanding, controlling, judgmental, intolerant, ruthless, overbearing, extravagant, and arrogant in the extreme. They usually get people to do what they want and become angry if they don't.

Famous Kings[6]

Alexander the Great, Mark Anthony, Diahann Carroll, Catherine the Great, Sean Connery, Elizabeth Dole, J. Paul Getty, Raisa Gorbachev, Katherine Hepburn, Linda Hunt, Jacqueline Kennedy Onassis, John F. Kennedy, Rose Kennedy, Madonna, Sandra Day O'Connor, Aristotle Onassis, Queen Elizabeth I, Richard the Lion-Hearted, Donald Trump, Katarina Witt.

Artisan

It is obvious from the name that this is a creative role among the seven aspects, but it is not true that all Artisans are "artists." Artisans may be found in numerous roles other than that of the performing or creative arts. They may be cooks, writers, project schedulers, carpenters, architects, linguists, hairdressers, waitresses, or ski instructors. They multitask by nature and tend to become bored quickly.

They make good salespeople, because they are like chameleons and adapt easily to change. They are adept at appearing like any other aspect and as such are natural actors. They often love the theater but can quickly tire of the roles they play.

The essence of the Artisan is her creativity, which manifests itself in the desire to bring about what has never been done before. Artisans achieve this through their inventiveness and engineering. The Artisan can apply her unique view of life to create new life forms and ideas the rest of the aspects find so intriguing. Artisans are the "spice" of life and both initiate and materialize the visions of the King.

An Artisan is likely to have the following thoughts running through her mind: *"What would this room be like if I painted it blue? Could I put a painting over there? I wonder how far it is to that star? I wonder what it would be like to travel through space. Oh, how I would love to fly. Let's see. How could I fly? I could create some wing...some wings out of...feathers and tie them together on some boards, strap them to my back, and fly. I could jump off the roof and take off. I could fly to the moon. I could fly to that star. I could fly! I know I could if I tried."*

"Oh, it's time to get ready to go. What shall I wear? Let's see these green and navy striped leggings are perfect with the platform sandals and this floral top. I think I'll put on this flower bracelet and braid my hair with butterfly bands. Perfect! I just need to look for something with a little more color next time I go to the store."

That would be a normal internal dialogue for an Artisan, a day-dreamer who is creative, always thinking up ideas, some of which may be impossible or improbable, but who knows, they just might discover something in the process.

Artisans need time alone. They need time to daydream, to explore. They need time to discover the wonders of life and dream up some that don't even exist yet. They are happier when left to their own de-sign and can be quite difficult to deal with in a deadline situation.

Artisans have a unique effect on group situations. They create an atmosphere. Their mere presence can enhance creativity without them even doing anything. Conversely, if an Artisan is unhappy or emotion-ally unavailable, the whole group may become blocked and not able to communicate with each other.

Artisans are expressively creative at all levels. They approach the whole world as if it is their canvas. Some of these expressions—tattoos, purple hair, or platform shoes—may seem bizarre to the rest of the world. They are the kind of people who become frustrated if they are not allowed to express their creativity. They will become blocked and upset. They need to express in order to stay healthy, both physically and emotionally.

In the business world, they may attack several issues at once—finance, scheduling, personnel, marketing—in a seemingly random fashion. Although it often works, sometimes they are not able to complete their tasks. This causes frustration with managers and coworkers of other aspects, such as Warriors, Kings, or Servers.

How Artisans Relate to Others

Artisans can find day-to-day life boring and may create dramas in order to alleviate the boredom. Because of this, they may be deceptive or manipulative and distort information merely to be creative or different. Rumors are most likely started by a bored Artisan.

They often have a difficult time being grounded and may appear spaced-out or disoriented. As a rule, they prefer working one-on-one rather than in large groups. They may be intimidated by crowds because their energy gets dispersed over a wider range. An exception to this is the actor who performs to audiences.

Artisans get along well with Storytellers. They enjoy the company of Priests and can relate to their more sacred view of life. They crave the creativity that comes with exploring the spiritual aspects of things and could expound on philosophy with Priests for hours on end.

Warriors, on the other hand, can intimidate Artisans, since they represent an opposite way of being. Warriors represent the physicality of life. Artisans hold a fear for the way the Warrior is solid, focused, and confronting. It follows that the Warrior confounds the gentle sensibilities of the Artisan.

Artisans generally resonate well with Kings. They would be well suited for partnerships in business or marriage. The Artisan enjoys the power and mastery associated with the King, and the King utilizes the creativity and artistry of the Artisan.

It is probable that a high percentage of Americans (estimated 34.5 percent)[7] are Artisans. They are quick to grasp ideas and as such are the pioneers of our time. By the time the rest of the world catches up with them, they are often already bored with the original idea and are on to something else. Because they are so far ahead of the other aspects, they often feel misunderstood. Sometimes Artisans find strength in numbers and will gravitate towards support groups or even communities of like people. (Santa Fe, New Mexico; Sedona, Arizona; San Francisco, California; Berkeley, California; Seattle, Washington; Minneapolis, Minnesota—all are cities with large populations of Artisans.)[8]

Artisans are the architects of civilization in that they create the ideas from which societies are built: democracy, socialism, the barter system.

Understandably, the Artisan aspect would be easier to express in today's Western society as a woman rather than a man. Western society allows women more freedom to express themselves creatively than it gives to men. It may be more of a struggle for a male Artisan to fully express his creativity and remain a "man" in the world's eyes.

Positive Characteristics of Artisans

Artisans are flexible, spontaneous, creative, visionaries, original, eccentric, dreamweavers, inventive, playful, catalysts for creativity within a group, the what-if person, chaos-producing (then the Warriors make sense of the chaos), and the ultimate yin. They see the big picture, "out there," and are not afraid of exploring possibilities.

Negative Characteristics of Artisans

Artisans can be spaced-out, confused, deceptive and manipulative, irresponsible, moody, self-indulgent, false, and impulsive. They disperse energy over a wide group of tasks and may not be able to complete any of them. They create their own negative reality if they so choose, which can lead to mental illness.

Famous Artisans[9]

Lynn Andrews, Marie Antoinette, Antonio Banderas, Drew Barrymore, Angela Bassett, Warren Beatty, Brian Boitano, Sandra Bullock, Nicholas Cage, Mary Cassatt, Cher, Sheryl Crow, Tom Cruise, Joan Cusack, Leonardo da Vinci, Geena Davis, Catherine Deneuve, Walt Disney, Paul Gauguin, Lady Godiva, Alexander Godunov, Hugh Grant, Germaine Greer, Melanie Griffith, Scott Hamilton, John Heard,

Jimi Hendrix, Whitney Houston, Iman, Chris Isaak, Michael Jackson, Thomas Jefferson, Nicole Kidman, Jessica Lange, Annie Lenox, George Lucas, Mary Stuart Masterson, Michelangelo, Joni Mitchell, Wolfgang Amadeus Mozart, Julia Ormond, Brad Pitt, Michelle Pfeiffer, Prince, Linda Rondstadt, Winona Ryder, Claudia Schiffer, Meryl Streep, James Taylor, Vincent Van Gogh, Andy Warhol, Walt Whitman, Frank Lloyd Wright, Kristi Yamaguchi, and my daughter, Audrey, whose creativity is expressed in everything she does, from outlandish clothing combinations to sculpture and music, and who elevates the dream-like state to an art form, especially when it comes time to go somewhere or do something she doesn't want to do.

Notice that the list for famous Artisans is greater than any other list. By their nature, Artisans are drawn to the performing arts and thereby gain celebrity through the media and entertainment industries.

Storyteller

As the name indicates, a Storyteller is someone who loves to relate to others by telling stories. They teach, entertain, coerce, and change the dynamics of situations through their vivid explanations of the world around them. They can be wise truth tellers or manipulate the truth as a means to an end. They do this all with honesty and sincerity and very much believe in themselves. In fact, when they do distort the truth, they are unaware that they are doing so. They rationalize. They reason that they are justified in all their words and deeds.

Therefore, a Storyteller is a powerful persuader. They entertain us with their stories. They teach us through anecdotes and delight us with their sprightly humor and their command of language. Even when we know they may be telling a white lie or distorting the truth, we love them anyway. We don't seem to care because they are forgiven. For in their human frailty, we see our own shortcomings and love them for it. They make us laugh.

Storytellers stand out in a crowd. They are charismatic, dramatic, witty, long-winded, and hilarious. They possess great wisdom, although sometimes the depth of their wisdom isn't readily apparent.

One interesting point to make when looking at the Storyteller aspect is that even though the Storyteller may have a "flawed" personality as far as telling the truth, it can often be among the wisest of all of the aspects. This aspect could be likened to the wise "old ones" of ancient tribes. Storytellers were the men and women who carried the oral tradition down through the ages; they were healers who worked their magic through ritual and the sage wisdom that could only come from an elder.

As a creative and expressive aspect, a Storyteller may often seem to be able to access wisdom beyond the here and now. It is as if they could reach across time and glean wisdom from the ages. The wonder of what they bring to life is in their uncanny ability to translate this wisdom into entertaining stories. This enables them to explain advanced concepts and principles to the masses. Witness movies such as *ET, Star Wars, Cocoon, What Dreams May Come,* and *Field of Dreams.* All of these movies and thousands of others, plus books, songs, plays, even commercials on TV are inspired by writers with a creative sense of story, access to greater wisdom than themselves, and the ability to convey this wisdom to the world.

How Storytellers Relate to Others

The Storyteller is the companion aspect to the Artisan. As mentioned before, they often combine to create artistic forms of expression that delight, entertain, and educate us. They work together to delight an audience. Because they enjoy being the center of attention they can become quite annoyed if ignored.

Storytellers can be slower to mature because they are so creative and fun loving. This can be frustrating for the aspects who take their roles much more seriously: a Priest, who wishes to inspire others; or to the Warrior and King, who are action oriented. Storytellers get along best with Artisans and Scholars. Scholars allow them to dump all of their words and stories onto them to store, catalogue, and even to organize. Warriors can become frustrated with Storytellers because of their creative "bending" of the truth, but both share a love for "rollicking fun."

The Storyteller and the Artisan are both on the Expressive Axis (see figure 1.1). However, the Storyteller is the broader focused of the two. The Artisan is more specifically focused. This indicates that the Storyteller falls into the directive leadership role, and the Artisan is content doing her own thing rather than directing others. Where Artisans express creativity through various mediums, Storytellers express their creativity with words, usually orally but also in written form. Storytellers often collaborate with Artisans to bring beauty, fun, and excitement to the world. Together they can be found creating films, plays, and music.

Storytellers gravitate towards professions such as acting, politics, sales, journalism, public speaking, news anchors, and advertising. They love the media. Their main focus is to make sure that information is conveyed in the best way possible to all parties that need to know. They fight for the freedom of expression and access to all newsworthy stories. They are adept at finding the angle, whether it be human interest, shock, or sympathetic insight. Their stories touch our hearts and activate our internal systems of awareness, change, and expression. In this way, they help us become better than ourselves. They inspire without meaning to. Growth through entertainment is their creed.

There are fewer Storytellers, as opposed to Artisans or Warriors, because fewer are needed in society. In comparison, about 11 percent of the population are Storytellers[10] as opposed to 34.5 percent Artisans, 24 percent Warriors, and 1.5 percent Kings.

Positive Characteristics of Storytellers

Storytellers are expressive, good with words, interesting, funny, witty, charming, persuasive, perceptive, humorous, entertaining, and knowledgeable. They have good leadership skills and can manage and direct others to action. They believe in teaching through fun and that life is to enjoy, not suffer.

Negative Characteristics of Storytellers

Storytellers can be deceitful, loud, vexing, attention-grabbing, blowhards, tasteless, crass, egocentric, gossipy, irresponsible, and wonderful sleazy characters. They may try to force their views upon you whether or not you're interested in hearing about them.

Famous Storytellers[11]

Bella Abzug, Dan Ackroyd, Kirstie Alley, Maya Angelou, Lucille Ball, Kathy Bates, John Belushi, Candice Bergen, Sandra Bernhard, Carol Burnett, George Carlin, Johnny Carson, Connie Chung, John Cleese, Cleopatra, Bill Clinton, Natalie Cole, Katie Couric, Cindy Crawford, Phyllis Diller, Fran Drescher, Olympia Dukakis, Patty Duke, Ella Fitzgerald, Betty Ford, Michael J. Fox, Betty Friedan, Teri Garr, Mel Gibson, Whoopi Goldberg, Valerie Harper, Goldie Hawn, Don Johnson, Janis Joplin, Diane Keaton, Ricki Lake, Ann Landers, Angela Lansbury, Jay Leno, David Letterman, Shirley MacLaine, Bill Murray, Jack Nicholson, Rosie O'Donnell, Sarah Jessica Parker, Dolly Parton, Eva Peron, Tim Robbins, Roseanne, RuPaul, Rene Russo, William Shakespeare, Dinah Shore, Carly Simon, Gary Sinese, Christian Slater, Solomon, Sting, Barbara Streisand, Kathleen Turner, Tina Turner, Mark Twain, Abigail Van Buren, Barbara Walters, Dr. Ruth Westheimer.

Server

Servers tend to be pleasers and are very approachable. They are modest and do what they do for others simply for their own satisfaction, not for praise or reward. They can often be found behind the scenes helping things to run smoothly and efficiently. Most often they are quiet in their methods and as such can sometimes be overlooked or under-appreciated.

It is sometimes difficult to spot a Server. Parental or societal conditioning can distort natural tendencies and make it look as if a person is a Server when, in essence, she really is not. Before the 1960s, children were to be "seen and not heard." Children were encouraged to assist with the family in any way possible—do chores, help with younger siblings, serve the family unit instead of meeting their own needs. This was easy for a Server, but would have been difficult for most of the other aspects.

Imagine a child who is: a King with the natural ability to lead, a Priest with the need to be in a leadership-consulting role, or a Storyteller with the desire to have fun and not to work too hard. These children would have been guided, directed, and encouraged to demonstrate Server tendencies and, in some cases, override their own basic personalities. They may have developed a "false personality" and not felt good about themselves in the process.

The '60s were a backlash against these and other societal pressures. Rebellion was the key word. All aspects were able to break loose and experience themselves in new ways. This was great for the other aspects, but difficult for Servers. Servers were no longer valued, but vehemently put down by the women's movement, workforces, and even their own children. "What are you, Mom, a *doormat?*" was the frequent mantra from children and therapists alike. Servers were confused and, in some cases, made themselves look like other aspects to survive. This may explain the role confusion for woman Servers born during the '30s and '40s who saw that society placed little value on their true selves. They experienced low self-esteem and bitterness without having an outlet for their desire to serve.

Fulfillment for each aspect comes from living the truth of herself as clearly and as honestly as possible. Servers who are truly Servers and not forced into the role can be spotted because there is no ego struggle. The other roles, with possibly the exception of Priest, have a difficult time putting their own egos aside and not pursuing their own agendas. When one's own agenda is involved in giving service to others, one sets up a situation to be in control. There may even be manipulation involved. A Server, in contrast, gives with no need for return, without manipulation.

How Servers Relate to Others

Why would anyone want to be a Server? The Server role is the same as the slave or serf in past societies. Now, since we have evolved into a society that has transcended the need for slavery, the Server role has fashioned into one of a facilitator. Servers put other people's needs before their own and, in doing so, facilitate their own spiritual growth. The fastest way to spiritual enlightenment is through selfless service to others.

Servers are excellent at behind the scenes control. In fact, taken to the extreme, Servers can be passive-aggressive. They love to assist in helping to unfold whatever scenario they deem to be the most appropriate. On the other hand, they have difficulty confronting people and prefer to be indirect, obtuse, and avoid rather than come face to face with a problem.

Servers have an eye for detail and a sense of timing. When they are not in control of a situation, they can feel frustrated, trapped, and enslaved. They have a hard time saying no and, as such, can become overworked and underpaid. They are often taken advantage of because of their willingness to be of service.

They enjoy professions such as physician, nurse, psychotherapist, teacher, full-time homemaker, waiter, butler, and other service people. They make it possible for the other aspects to be who they truly are by: healing them when they're hurt, providing food when they are hungry, and sheltering them when they need a place to stay. Servers are the backbones of society, and the other aspects would have a difficult time fulfilling their destinies without them.

The Server is the specific-focused aspect between the two Inspiration aspects of Priest and Server. A Priest is more outwardly directed. A Server prefers to work individually with people and leave the direction of groups of people to the Priests, Kings, and Storytellers.

Historically, Servers constituted about 30 percent of the population and were the most numerous of all the aspects.[12] More recently, however, since the 1960s, Servers have dwindled to about 6 percent of the population. Artisans, at 34.5 percent, are the most numerous. Warriors, at 24 percent, were the dominant aspect; however, over the last two years, it has shifted to Artisans. A true Server is much harder to find in today's society. This is true not only of the United States, but of most of the developed countries as well.

In the past, Servers were needed because they were the backbone of society and did most of the work. As technology quickens our daily existence and we enter into ever-increasing rates of change, the Server energy lessens in importance, especially in the United States. The majority of Servers who are now in the United States are over fifty years old. Servers are found today in great numbers in India and China.

Interestingly, a famous or more visible person could be a Server, for example, Queen Elizabeth II or Eleanor Roosevelt. Although they like to stay in the background, they are sometimes forced into positions of power and prominence.

Positive Characteristics of Servers

Servers are nurturing, caring, sympathetic, healing, hardworking, efficient, thorough, quiet, unassuming, devoted, friendly, loyal, trustworthy, honest, and ethical. They facilitate and achieve spiritual growth through selfless service to others.

Negative Characteristics of Servers

Servers can be passive-aggressive, weak, manipulative, controlling, domineering, covert, underhanded, overextended, martyred, overwhelmed, afraid or unable to set clear boundaries, and pleasers. They may fail to see appropriate time and place for energy to be directed to the most appropriate activities, places, and/or people. They may act like a victim or a doormat.

Priest

The Priest is the companion aspect to the Server. Both exist to inspire others, but the Priest has a more outward-directed focus. The Priest teaches, ministers, and leads others with zeal and charisma.

A Priest looks at the larger picture and as such is a visionary. She leads with conviction. A Priest could likely be found as the newly hired person to lead a poorly managed company back to better times. They have the ability to galvanize the "troops" and bind them together to work towards a common cause. A Priest would delight in the challenge of bringing a bankrupt enterprise out of the "red" and into the "black." She would keep the larger vision in mind while orchestrating each action towards the end goal.

A Priest would make a good team coach or project team leader. They have the ability to inspire others by getting them to "buy" into their vision, then rally their followers into giving their all to assure that the vision is realized. In return, they give their followers a sense of purpose.

There are few Priests in the total population: about 9 percent because only a few are needed. As an inspiring leader, the Priest stands out in a crowd. Much like the King, the old adage of "we need fewer chiefs and more Indians" applies. Not everyone can lead. If the world consisted only of leaders, who would be left for them to lead? Therefore, Priests are the charismatic, inspirational leaders much in the mode of Princess Diana, Oprah Winfrey, or Joan of Arc.

Priests are high-energy. They drive themselves and their bodies with unbelievable ferocity. They are more fluid in thoughts and motions than the other aspects and as such appear to be extremely flexible and quick to adapt. They may go to bed late at night and still rise early in the morning. Multitasking is no problem for Priests; it is a way of life.

A sense of mission or purpose, drives the Priest. A Priest will be working toward some greater goal. People will flock to them for advice and direction on spiritual and personal matters. It is easy to be caught up in their dream, so much so that others may have trouble setting their own boundaries when faced with the zeal of a Priest.

Witness Joan of Arc, a charismatic Priest. She fearlessly fought for her vision and inspired others to unite with her to fulfill her dream. She inspired men and women. Both volunteered to carry out tasks for her even before asked. Young King Charles and her protector Jean de Metz were in awe of her innocent yet fierce conviction to her beliefs. They were among the influential people who fell under her spell and helped her fulfill her destiny.

As a child, she possessed such power and sense of destiny that she threatened her own father, who shunned her from the family because he didn't understand. The "fathers" of the Catholic Church were intimidated by the purity and truth of her vision, and she was eventually put to death. But before this happened, she faced the humanness of her own nature and through ego and tunnel vision led many of her soldiers to their deaths. She was a catalyst for change, but her zealousness got in the way of being able to see clearly. True to the nature of the Priest, she led with energy and charisma so much so that her legend lives to this day.

In a way, Priests are salespeople. They sell others on their vision and use emotions to carry out their purpose. They work quickly, as if there isn't enough time to achieve everything there is to achieve. They thrive on the agonies and ecstasies of life and thrill to experience the higher states of emotions themselves. In religious terms, they would revel in being bathed in the Holy Spirit or to be in a meditative state.

They prefer to experience the higher forms of intellectual reasoning and philosophy through their emotions.

This can be illustrated in the Priest's personality as both positive or negative. Positive examples can be seen in Joan of Arc's courageous call to arms against the English and Princess Diana's zeal to champion the less fortunate, from AIDS patients to land mine victims. The world was mesmerized by Diana, continually hungry for tidbits about her life. She became an international icon through the media and transfixed the world with her inspirational qualities.

Negative examples of Priests using their power can be found in Rasputin, the Russian zealot Priest, and Adolf Hitler, the horribly destructive charismatic leader of World War II.

A Priest operates at a higher energy and frequency level than the other aspects. A violin is a wonderfully complex instrument. Tuned and played under skillful hands, it makes heavenly sounds. When out of tune and in less skilled hands, it sounds like a donkey braying, cacophonous and rude. Someone with the Priest as her Primary Aspect will perform at her highest level when coming from a more mature, sage place. A Priest who is immature is dangerous and can lead others down a path of misery, as seen by the example of Hitler and Rasputin.

How Priests Relate to Others

Sometimes Priests can be overzealous, so obsessed with their own goals that they lose sight of the needs of their followers. They can be abusive and invade the boundaries of those that they lead. They also can be so focused on achieving their goal that they overlook inaccuracies and bend the truth. They are impulsive and at times impractical. This historically has led to great genius as well as crushing defeat. One need look no further than the battles led by Joan of Arc. As brilliant and victorious as her initial battles were, the latter ones were marred by her impulsiveness and naiveté. She believed herself to be above the law of man, that she could achieve victory by her communion with God and Saint Catherine, but in the end she fell victim to false pride and narrow-mindedness, very human and priestly characteristics.

As this example demonstrates, a Warrior may not trust a Priest because of the Priest's quickness to act, which could put others at risk for the sake of achieving their goals. Priests get along well with Servers, Artisans, and Scholars. Servers help them fulfill their goals. Artisans also are visionaries and operate at a higher frequency level. Scholars are able to record, assimilate, and organize their ideas. This is essential in order for them to bring their ideas to the masses. Therefore, Priests must become adept at utilizing the media. They must also be careful to select the appropriate person (i.e., aspect) to aid them in achieving their goal.

Priests make excellent healers and can use their deep compassion to help others heal emotionally, spiritually, as well as physically. As illustrated by the tremendous sacrifice and dedication shown by Aung San Suu Kyi, the people's hero and political activist in Burma who was under house arrest from 1989 to 1995. She has dedicated her life to giving her people hope that they can overcome the tyranny of dictatorship and can Westernize to have a democracy, freedom of choice, and a capitalistic economy. She threatens the status quo, has been persecuted to the full extent of the military powers currently in control, and has been a martyr for the cause.

Priests tend to be the most political of the other roles; therefore, they are quicker than other aspects to grasp an opening, an opportunity to gain power or control, and can use this in a big way for the greater good of their community or for their own personal power.

Positive Characteristics of Priests

Priests are visionaries, compassionate, healers, caring, charismatic, and globally oriented. They have an appreciation of what the masses want and need and the ability to help others achieve a higher purpose. They also have a sense of purpose or mission and the ability to rally and lead others.

Negative Characteristics of Priests

Priests can be overzealous, evangelical, flaky, reactionaries, bigoted, and manipulative. They may possess tunnel vision and have no trouble using others to acheve their goal possibly to the detriment of others. They may want to fix everything whether or not it is asked or wanted and may force their beliefs on others.

Famous Priests[14]

Joan Baez, Jim Bakker, Jane Campion, Kevin Costner, Marie Curie, Princess Diana, Bob Dylan, Mahatma Gandhi, Woody Guthrie, Audrey Hepburn, Adolf Hitler, Jesse Jackson, Joan of Arc, Carl Jung, Helen Keller, Coretta Scott King, Ben Kingsley, Aung San Suu Kyi, Malcolm X, Thomas Merton, Rosa Parks, Priscilla Presley, Ayn Rand, Nancy Reagan, Oral Roberts, Pat Robertson, Anita Roddick, Diane Sawyer, Phyllis Schlafly, Martin Sheen, Bernie Siegel, Susan Sontag, St. Francis of Assisi, Jessica Tandy, Lily Tomlin, Lao Tze, Janine Turner, Denzel Washington, Sigourney Weaver, Marianne Williamson, Oprah Winfrey, Debra Winger, Stevie Wonder.

Scholar

According to our model of the seven aspects, the Scholar is the only aspect considered to be neutral. It is neither broadly nor specifically focused. A Scholar is the middle ground between all aspects, and as such can communicate easily with any of them. A Scholar's focus is detached, much like the journalist whose sole goal is to find the "who, what, when, where, and why" of a story. Her main function is to assimilate and record information and experiences so that all aspects can learn from what she has gathered.

The telltale sign of a Scholar is the degree of her detachment from the intense emotional swings of the other aspects. That is not to say that they don't experience emotions such as envy, sadness, and anger, but that they keep their emotions in check enough to render a more neutral response. They are less likely to be "hooked" than a Warrior, who tends to have antennae out looking for trouble.

A Scholar feels at home being at the center of the activity of the other aspects. They like to feel depended upon for clarity, mediation, and as a voice of reason. A good example would be Mr. Spock, the Vulcan character from the *Star Trek* television series. He remained detached yet provided valuable information to the crew of the Starship Enterprise. Judges, writers, and professors are often Scholars.

Examples of women Scholars include Gloria Steinem, Jodie Foster, Jane Goodall, Jane Bryant Quinn, Faith Popcorn (the forecaster), Margaret Mead, and Dianne Feinstein. Examples of male Scholars include Aristotle, Joseph Campbell, Carlos Castenada, Michael Crichton, Al Gore, and Alan Greenspan.

How Scholars Relate to Others

Scholars make excellent mediators. Neutrality is a key word for them. When a Scholar is present, the other aspects have an easier time communicating. Therefore, it would be helpful when planning a meeting or resolving conflicts to have a Scholar on hand. They process information differently. They take the time to gather information first, then sort it and organize it into useful categories. When presented with a problem between two "warring" factions, a Scholar would first seek all pertinent information from both sides. While doing this, she would be careful to only keep information that was necessary to come to a resolution (i.e., not past problems, or speculation about what could happen. "Just the facts, Ma'am."). After this fact gathering, she would take time to think it through and render an impartial solution to both parties. This process sounds remarkably like what a judge does when trying a case in the courtroom, and is indicative of the way the mind of the Scholar works.

This is not to say that the Scholar is a dry, dull personality. To the contrary, because the Scholar has the ability to be detached, she is less likely to be a "pleaser" and more likely to be happy with herself. This allows her the freedom to express her feelings without reprisal. So if she wants to play a practical joke on someone, she will, without worrying about what the other person would think of her. For example, it is well known that Jodie Foster, a Scholar, is a great practical joker. She continually comes up with outrageous, humiliating stunts to pull on co-stars when she is doing a movie with them. She laughs and "cuts up" yet still has an air of detachment, almost a scholarly aloofness. It is endearing to see her when she is laughing and telling about the practical jokes she pulls because it helps us to see her "humanness," to break through the neutral exterior and show us her emotional side.

Scholars are best at hindsight judgments. They carry out their functions of recording, assimilating, and analyzing better after a situation has occurred rather than visualizing for the future. They make great historians and are adept at synthesizing the facts to help make scientific, credible predictions of the future rather than fantasizing about what may happen. Faith Popcorn, a well-known prediction theorist, utilizes Scholar techniques to make her predictions. She extrapolates data from the past to infer the likely possibilities for the future.

Scholars are curious. They are driven by a need to know. They may select one subject and dedicate themselves to studying it forever. No matter whether they choose to study fossils from the Ordovician Era, a single genus of the plant kingdom, or gorillas in the wilds of Africa, the topic interests them to the distraction of all else. They can spend the rest of their lives studying this one topic.

This being said, they also possess a love for adventure. They have the courage to pioneer a cause or to pursue the study of a new topic. In this, they share something in common with a Warrior, who also possesses a love for adventure and the courage to explore. The difference lies in that a Scholar seeks adventure out of curiosity, and a Warrior seeks adventure out of a craving for new challenges and action. Scholars and Warriors make good companions. They are both well-grounded and physically active. Scholars can endure extreme climates, but also tend to experience more aches and pains than other aspects. They tend to hold information and experiences in their bodies and must consciously release them in order to heal. For example, a Scholar may have muscle or neck spasms or stomach problems and will have to unload some of the tension brought on by information overload before she can feel better.

Scholars enjoy a wide variety of experiences. They usually switch careers several times and enjoy various hobbies and interests.

About 12 percent of the population could be considered to be

Scholars.[15] They are drawn to professions such as philosophy, history, and science and are happiest when teaching, researching, and have access to large amounts of information.

Positive Characteristics of Scholars

Scholars are organized, good at mediating, neutral, knowledgeable, thorough, practical, grounded, curious, excellent observers, logical, and adventurous. They value clarity, like to pioneer new theories and teachings, and help to teach through recording mistakes and showing others how to learn from them.

Negative Characteristics of Scholars

Scholars can be so logical that they show no emotion, abstract, theoretical, tedious, boring, arrogant, too neat, and withdrawn. In the worst case, a Scholar may act like she is knowledgeable about something when she is only gathering theories about it. She may even fool herself into thinking that she really is the authority on the topic. The Scholar may have a sense of control but not based on truth.

Famous Scholars [16]

Aristotle, Jane Brody, Jane Bryant Quinn, Joseph Campbell, Carlos Castenada, Michael Crichton, Claire Danes, Robert Dole, Diane English, Dianne Feinstein, Dian Fossey, Jodie Foster, Bridget Fonda, Galileo, Jane Goodall, Al Gore, Germaine Greer, Raul Julia, John Lennon, Margaret Mead, Bill Moyers, Nostradamus, Sylvia Plath, Plato, Cokie Roberts, Greta Sacchi, Susan Sarandon, Socrates, Gertrude Stein, Gloria Steinem, Margaret Thatcher.

Each Woman Is a "Sisterhood" of Three Aspects

Now that you have uncovered your aspects, read the following for more detail about characteristics of your aspects and how each aspect relates to the other.

Each woman is an individual made up of many components. These components or aspects combine to influence your emotions and your interactions with others who in turn possess their own unique combination of aspects. An individual is a "sisterhood" of three aspects. The more she is at peace with her own aspects, the more she can be at peace with the aspects of others. When a woman's aspects are not "in sync" within herself or with others, conflicts arise.

FIGURE 1.4

Individual (Internal Sisterhood)

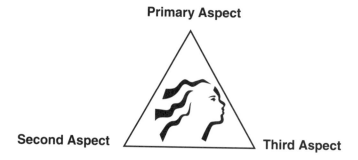

Primary Aspect

Second Aspect　　　　**Third Aspect**

The **Primary Aspect** corresponds to the most prominent personality traits you portray to people.

The **Second Aspect** is the counterpoint or complement to the Primary. It doesn't have to be the exact opposite, but can be complementary. So that a Warrior doesn't have to have a King secondary aspect, or an Artisan may have a different secondary aspect than a Storyteller. The Second Aspect instead is a way of adding complexity and rounding out one's personality.

For example, an Artisan-Priest could be someone who is creative and dreamy, but who also is interested in looking at the deeper meaning in her art. She may be drawn to expressing her deeper Priest side through her art or in her relationships with other people. A Warrior-Server is someone who is active, perhaps an athlete; organized; and driven but who wouldn't hesitate to drop everything to help someone in need. She is someone who would volunteer to build a house for Habitat for Humanity, deliver meals to shut-ins, and then stay to clean their house for them. She has tons of energy and intuitively gives where needed.

The **Third Aspect (Tertiary)** is subtle and serves as the link for the personality to relate to the greater family of the other aspects. It can be thought of as the "family name." For example, a King-Artisan-Scholar would be someone who loves to be in positions of authority, is artistic by nature (perhaps expresses this as a hobby rather than as a profession), but who is a rational, intelligent thinker. This person resonates with the "scholarliness" of other Scholars and enjoys stimulating intellectual conversation, but she doesn't necessarily show it in all of her interactions with others. The first two aspects would be more predominate.

A Scholar-Warrior-Priest is a woman who loves to read and write, but also is active. Most likely an adventure seeker, she would also be looking for some deeper meaning or inspiration while she was reading and seeking the adventure. She could therefore most likely be a rock climber who writes for a magazine or a professor who travels to far-away mystic places.

An Example of Putting Aspects to Work for You

As you read the following explanations of the aspects in greater detail, the significance of self-discovery will be apparent. Let's look at one possible combination. Athena is a Warrior-Scholar-Artisan (see figure 1.5). How can she put this information to work in her relationships?

FIGURE 1.5

Athena: Example of a Possible Combination

Warrior (Primary Aspect)

Scholar
(Second Aspect)

Artisan
(Third Aspect)

If Athena is trying to coordinate efforts at work or for a volunteer organization and a few women are being resistant, she could ascertain how to gain their cooperation by drawing inferences about their aspects. As a Warrior, Athena is a good organizer and often a leader. She is not motivated by power, but the satisfaction that the job is done right.

If the women who are giving her problems are primarily Kings, Priests, or Storytellers, the main issue could be power. These three aspects crave the spotlight and need to feel recognized for what they do. If this is the case, Athena could work to gain their cooperation by allowing them the power and recognition they crave in return for completing the task at hand. She could do this by forming small groups and appointing them to be leaders. She could ask for their opinion, and give them positive feedback in front of the group. She could give them power to expedite the process. Instead of escalating the conflict, Athena uses creativity to facilitate change. If the process is stuck, she will be able to get it moving. This is a win-win situation. In addition to getting the task completed, she goes a long way towards improving communication between women. Women are empowered in the process, and it helps communication to spiral upward towards personal growth instead of deteriorating into gossip and conflict.

Famous Women: What Aspects Are They?

King-Warrior-Priest	Elizabeth Dole
King-Warrior-Artisan	Katherine Hepburn
King-Artisan-Storyteller	Madonna
Warrior-Storyteller-Scholar	Chris Evert
Warrior-King-Priest	Sharon Stone
Warrior-Storyteller-King	Gertrude Stein
Storyteller-Priest-King	Whoopi Goldberg
Storyteller-Artisan-King	Barbara Walters
Storyteller-Priest-King	Maya Angelou
Storyteller-King-Artisan	Sark
Priest-Artisan-King	Oprah Winfrey
Priest-Storyteller-King	Audrey Hepburn
Priest-Server-Warrior	Rosa Parks
Priest-Warrior-King	Aung San Suu Kyi
Priest-Artisan-Server	Princess Diana
Scholar-Priest-Storyteller	Faith Popcorn
Scholar-Priest-Warrior	Jodie Foster
Scholar-Priest-Storyteller	Cokie Roberts
Artisan-Priest-Storyteller	Faith Hill
Artisan-Priest-Server	Joni Mitchell
Artisan-Priest-King	Catherine Deneuve
Artisan-Storyteller-Warrior	Melanie Griffith
Server-King-Storyteller	Eleanor Roosevelt
Server-Priest-King	Mother Teresa
Server-Artisan-Scholar	Laura Dern

It is fascinating to look at these combinations. Notice the first two Kings are the same King-Warrior combination, but differ with the Third Aspect. Elizabeth Dole with the tertiary aspect of Priest shows her tendency to be inspirational to others in her role as head of the Red Cross. Katherine Hepburn shows her tertiary aspect of Artisan through her dedication to the craft of acting. Both powerful women have the drive and will (Warrior) to lead with excellence (King), but chose to act with their environments in very different ways (tertiary aspects). Their Third Aspects take them into different expressions of their personal power.

Also note the Primary Artisan Aspects. The first three are all Artisan-Priest, which complement each other well. They inspire using creativity, but express it differently in the ways they react with their environments. Faith Hill sings her expressive nature and shows her tertiary aspect of Storyteller through stories in song, and the way she has fun with the media and videos. Also a singer and songwriter, Joni Mitchell (a Server) differs in her reaction with her environment because she likes to keep a lower profile. During the height of her popularity, she preferred to remain behind the scenes, and only became visible to promote a cause. Catherine Deneuve follows in the same track as an Artisan-Priest, but differs from the other two women in that her Third Aspect is King. This adds the element of a powerful presence, someone noticeable, someone people will look up to. She commands that presence through her acting and influences people around the world with her sense of artistry, style, and grace.

It is also possible to look at combinations as a couple.

Couple Combinations

It is interesting to note combinations of couples and how they illustrate the complementary nature of the aspects.

Joanne Woodward   **Storyteller-Warrior-King**

Paul Newman   **Warrior-Storyteller-Artisan**

With their Primary and Secondary Aspects as image twins, Woodward and Newman complement each other well. They differ only with the Third Aspect. Although Newman has been more visible in the outer world of entertainment than Woodward, she has carried her power and presence into their family. An accomplished actress in her own right, Woodward made a choice to put her energy (a King choice) into caring for her family. She did it in a "behind the scenes" manner as a powerful matriarch of the Newman family. Later in life, she attended college at the same time as her daughter and graduated with honors. She supported Newman's career, but in every acting role she played, her power and artistry showed. She exudes power and grace, and one has the sense in watching her that she is confidently following her own dreams and is greatly admired by her family.

FIGURE 1.7

The Seven Aspects Model

INSPIRATION	Aspect	Goal	Stumbling Block
Specific Focus	+Service **SERVER** -Frustration	+Simplicity **Re-evaluation** -Withdrawal	+Humility **Self-deprecation** -Abasement
Broad Focus	+Compassion **PRIEST** -Zeal	+Evolution **Growth** -Confusion	+Pride **Arrogance** -Vanity
EXPRESSION			
Specific Focus	+Creation **ARTISAN** -Self-deprecation	+Sophistication **Discrimination** -Rejection	+Sacrifice **Self-destruction** -Suicidal
Broad Focus	+Dissemination **STORYTELLER** -Oration	+Unconditional love **Acceptance** -Ingratiation	+Appetite **Greed** -Voracity
ACTION			
Specific Focus	+Persuasion **WARRIOR** -Coercion	+Devotion **Submission** -Subservience	+Selflessness **Martyrdom** -Victimization
Broad Focus	+Mastery **KING** -Tyranny	+Leadership **Dominance** -Dictatorship	+Daring **Impatience** -Intolerance
ASSIMILATION			
Neutral	+Knowledge **SCHOLAR** -Hypothesis	+Free flowing **Relaxation** -Inertia	+Determination **Stubbornness** -Obstinacy

Note: This is the complete personality model. It shows the negative and positive characteristics of each aspect, goal, and stumbling block. Stumbling blocks are discussed in chapter 4, and goals are discussed in chapter 5.

CHAPTER TWO

THE HEROINE'S JOURNEY: PART I

First We Learn To Live With Ourselves

"It's time that we rediscover passion
So we can feel this world again
Oh deep denial you're the dragon
And we're the fragile living things"

MICHAEL TOMLINSON
Excerpted from "Living Things"
1991 song from the Living Things CD

IT ISN'T EASY TO LEARN TO LIVE WITH OURSELVES. So many things get in the way. A close friend of mine has an excuse shirt for tennis. On it are various phrases such as: "It's too windy. Too hot. Too cold. You didn't hit the ball the way I like it. I'm too tired. Had too much coffee. Couldn't see it. The ball was too hard. Too slow." We have a good laugh when we read it, but I wonder how many times we create excuses in our lives instead of owning that the buck stops with us. There really are no excuses or victims when we realize we are the solution to our own problems.

The task of learning to live with ourselves is a grand journey we take starting with our first awareness that we have an impact on our environment. Many writers have written about the act of making it through life as being a hero's or heroine's journey. From personal experiences, observations, research, and work, the remaining chapters invite you to think about and consciously create your own journey. You may resonate with some of the examples, such as tennis or work, or you may find them different from your personal experience. The point is to take the ideas and themes and use them in your own way.

Jean Houston, a noted philosopher and writer of modern mythology, along with Joseph Campbell have written of the hero's/heroine's journey as having two great works to perform. The first is to withdraw from everyday life to reach an inner source of strength. The second is to come back into society to share the wisdom from your experience for use in our daily lives.

This process or journey is not painless. It usually begins with some call to adventure. The amazing part is that the call isn't always clear. Of course, it is easy to hear when it comes in the form of sickness, death of a loved one, divorce, loss of job, but even then we have to pay attention. It is not often that we hear a voice saying, "Hey, time to wake up. This is important. It's time to start your adventure!" Normally, we make a simple mistake, do something wrong, say the wrong thing to someone, break a promise. Or we make an immense mistake such as marrying the wrong person, taking the wrong job, or doing something we view as terrible. After we work through the guilt and depression, we may be ready to do something about it.

The heroine part of this process is that you take on all kinds of challenges you didn't know you could previously handle, until you reach the very depths or inner core of yourself. It is here where you can gain an insight or discover a skill that is a miraculous treasure. Then, as the heroine, you carry this treasure back with you into the world. The second part of the heroine's journey is carrying the wisdom back and putting it to use.

> You cannot stay on the summit forever; you have
> to come down. So why bother in the first
> place?
> Just this: What is above knows what is below,
> but what is below does not know what is
> above.
>
> In climbing, take careful note of the difficulties
> along your way for as you go up, you can
> observe them.
> Coming down, you will no longer see them, but
> will know they are there if you have observed
> them well.
>
> There is an art of conducting oneself in the
> lower regions by the memory of what one saw
> higher up.
> When one can no longer see, one can at least
> still know.
>
> RENE DUMAL
> *(French mountaineer)*
> *Mount Analogue*

For women, especially in these times, this journey is different. We experience this journey as how it is connected to what we know. It has value for us if we can share and use it in our relationships. While the mythic hero may have been content with coming back from his quest and receiving honors, the female heroine is a new myth who wants to come back and use her knowledge, along with men, to improve family relationships, help children, help other women, make social reforms, even contribute to world peace.

Each woman has her own journey and in order to be part of a strong, seamless sisterhood, it is important for her to pause and learn to listen to her inner voice. In this and subsequent chapters, suggestions and exercises are provided to help you more consciously experience your journey. Each reader is invited to explore her part of the sisterhood and honor that she is a unique and important member of the group. If every woman did this, I believe we could achieve the impossible—living harmoniously, accomplishing all that we need to do and more to live in peace.

When we think about changing the world, it becomes overwhelming. In the long run, all we can change is ourselves. We only have control of what we do, what we think, and where we direct our own energy.

Getting To Know Your Inner Self

> We cannot lead someone to the light when we
> are standing in the dark.
>
> CELEBRATING WOMEN

One of the best means of listening to your inner voice is to spend quiet time alone. It is difficult to listen to your intuition when distracted by problems and activities around you. So find a quiet place where you can spend uninterrupted time for at least thirty minutes to an hour.

You may find that you need to "unload" the baggage of the day or of thoughts in your mind. It is helpful to clear your mind of unwanted material so that you can focus your full attention on listening to your inner voice. Some people find it helpful to stretch or do exercises before they are ready to relax. Some find it beneficial to write to clear their mind, and some use breathing techniques. Whichever method you choose, be patient and keep with it. Don't expect miracles over night. It takes practice to be able to focus and not get carried away by distractions.

EXERCISE

Getting To Know Your Inner Self

Read the instructions before beginning the exercise. If possible, record them on a tape player or memorize them so you won't have to break your relaxation to read.

Find a comfortable spot. Sit tall. Imagine a helium balloon is attached to the top of your head and is pulling on your head, neck, and spine as it rises. Shoulders are relaxed and dropped, not hunched around your ears. Chest is expanded, and spine is straight. Visualize sitting and being pulled up from the base of your spine, while remaining firmly rooted to the floor. Breathe deeply and slowly.

Let thoughts and emotions pass. Watch them as they float by. Imagine that you are rock, a tall mountain. The wind is blowing all around you, blowing away all thoughts and cares. As it blows around you, it caresses and cleanses. No worries. They are blown away. Thoughts pass. No plans. Time stands still. You have nothing to do but breathe. (Let time pass to relax into this moment.)

Now that you are feeling relaxed, notice your breath. Lengthen your inhale and exhale. Slow your breathing. Take the breath deeper and expand your lungs. Focus only on your breath. (Continue for several minutes).

If you wish to go deeper into your relaxation, begin to breathe in a pattern. The count should be equal counts for each inhale, holding the breath, and exhale (for example, inhale for five counts, hold your breath for five counts, then exhale for five counts). This will take practice. The breath needs to be inhaled and exhaled uniformly over the five counts not in short erratic bursts. It is an even, flowing breath. Once you have mastered this breathing technique, you may vary the count if you wish (some people do as little as two counts; some do as many as twenty counts). The important part of the technique is the pattern and keeping the count the same for all three parts.

As you continue this breathing pattern, you will find yourself slipping deeper and deeper into relaxation. At some point, when you feel that you are totally relaxed and have let go of all thoughts and tension, you may stop focusing on your breath. Breathe normally.

At this point, notice how you feel. Are you holding tension in any part of your body? If so, note it and try to imagine your breath relaxing the tension away. Does your body feel light? Do you feel peaceful? Allow your body to relax into the peacefulness that surrounds you. Let it cradle you. Relax into the sensation that you are being cared for.

It is now time to get acquainted with your inner voice.

Imagine you are taking a long walk. The place is special and only yours. It may be a sunlit garden path or a comforting, enclosed tunnel through a warm cave. You are walking. Note anything unique or special along the way. It is a long walk, but soon you reach an opening.

You find yourself in a clearing. Off to the back is a small pool of water. Walk over to the pool and lean over, peering into the mirrored surface. As you gaze at the reflection, take careful note of the image reflected back to you. What does it look like?

After you have gazed at the reflection, ask it any question you wish: "What is your name?" "Do you have anything to tell me?" "Can you help me with___?" "What can I do about this problem?"

You don't have to speak the words out loud, say them in your mind. Be patient with yourself and your inner voice. It may take time for your inner voice to respond. If you keep asking questions and don't get any response, ask about that also. You may ask your voice to speak louder so you can hear. Your voice may respond to you with humor and unpredictable images or words. Make mental notes and go on.

Spend as much time as you wish getting to know your

inner self. Then when you feel that you have exhausted your questions and finished your time together, say thank you. Ask your inner self if it has a special name, voice, or means for you to make contact with it in the future. Ask if it has a token or gift to help you stay connected with it (i.e., a crystal, song, image, or word). Take careful note of this. Commit it to memory. Honor that you are being directed towards your higher good.

After you have thanked your inner self and said good-bye, turn and walk out of the clearing through the path by which you came and back to your starting point. As you reach the starting point, you begin to feel consciousness again. You begin to feel your toes, your arms, legs, hands. Your mind clears and you become alert, aware of what is going on around you. You awaken to be present in this time and space, yet remember clearly what has just transpired.

Before going on to your day-to-day tasks, take time to write your experiences. Write any thoughts, images, and messages your higher self may have given you. This is important for several reasons. First, you will forget some of the details if you don't record them right away. Second, it will be easier for you to connect with your intuitive inner voice next time if you honor the information it gave you this time by taking the time to write it down. Although the information is fresh and vivid at the present time, it will become blurred and perhaps forgotten as time passes.

Make sure that you are fully present before you go on to perform any tasks, especially ones that require full attention such as driving. This exercise is powerful and must be used as medicine—with respect in its proper time and place.

You may return to this place time and time again. You may discover other ways of getting in touch with your higher self. All of them will be okay as long as you are approaching the exercise with the intent of your higher good and as long as you ask for protection before each exercise so that you will be safe as you do any of the exercises.

Here is an example of a protection prayer:

Dear Heavenly Father (Mother, God),

May the glory of your love surround and protect me. Within your will and for my highest good, I ask for help in seeing things more clearly. Please lift the burden of negativity from me. Purify me through Christ's love. Help me to hear what I need to hear and see what I need to see. For this blessing I give thanks. Amen.

Write down any responses to your questions. This is important both to remember them and to say to yourself, "I value the information you have given me." It will be much easier to have your questions answered later if you honor the process now. You may have questions about your future, your aspect, or problems you are currently facing. Ask, listen, and record. This will help you come to an understanding about yourself and make it easier to use this information in the future.

The next time you go for a chat with your inner self the rendezvous point may look different. That's okay. It is not essential that the method remain the same. You just need to find what works for you. A reflective underground cavern pool may work for some people. For others, they may need a sunlit, high country meadow stream lined with spring flowers. The point is that whatever you get is right for you and special for you. Trust that you have the tools for personal growth already inside you. It is just a matter of unlocking the doors to those tools.

Exploring Your Uniqueness

For us to understand how we fit into the glass window of the sisterhood, we need to explore our uniqueness and clearly understand how that uniqueness affects our relationships. We need to understand our "piece" as it interacts with other "pieces."

Discovering your aspect is one way of looking at your uniqueness. Getting in touch with your inner voice or higher self is another. By trusting your own innate ability to heal or be the best you can be, you will become free from the distortions society and other people place on you. This will help your own internal barometer or internal guidance system let you know how you feel, when you have had enough of a situation, and what will bring you the most happiness and inner peace. It is better if this comes from within. As you begin to trust yourself, the wisdom of your inner voice will become easier to recognize and understand.

I know, from personal experience, that finding your true self—your uniqueness—and becoming comfortable enough to trust it is not an easy or quick process.

As a child, I was raised to be a Server or Artisan. My parents told me to put others first and do for others. They told me that the Christian way was to give and "turn the other cheek." They gave me messages that "girls weren't supposed to be good in sports" when I clumsily failed at running in PE class and encouraged me to do well in school, play the piano, and do creative things such as sew and pursue art projects. I listened and excelled at all of these things, but somehow felt incomplete. I felt anxious and limited, like a caged mustang with energy bristling just under the surface ready to come out.

I found an outlet for some of this energy in sampling a wider variety of activities: dance, drama, student council, learning French, and playing baseball with my family. Baseball was the only sport I was encouraged to do—and then I could only toss the ball with my father and brother in the backyard. I was never permitted to actually play on a team myself; that was left to the boys.

I was the last child picked for gym teams at school, and one of my biggest shames was that I was a slow runner and was deathly afraid of swimming. In junior high, I began to gain weight. I read voraciously and usually ate while I was reading. I had no physical activity and felt extremely anxious inside.

By the time I reached high school, my mother was saying things like, "You're not heavy, just pleasantly plump," and "Perhaps you should just have salad tonight for dinner, dear." My self-image as well as my body image were distorted. I didn't know who I was even though everyone else thought I was confident and self-assured.

I started crash dieting and exercising in high school and eventually was able to lose weight. At that point, I liked to lose weight so much that I couldn't stop and carried the cycle of anorexia and bulimia until well after college. I was a Warrior who was directed and imprinted by social conditioning to be something contrary to my inner nature. My inner voice was crying out to be heard, and I didn't even know enough to listen.

Because I am a Warrior-Scholar-Priest, I did find satisfaction in school, reading, and intellectual endeavors (Scholar) as well as being the leader in whatever activity I took on (Priest). I was interested in philosophy, psychology, and spiritual matters (Priest) and was always looking for the deeper meaning of things, yet I was at a loss to curb the restlessness and anxiety that lay beneath my surface.

It wasn't until well into my undergraduate years of college that I became comfortable with exercising and began to feel better about my body and myself. I started running, and somehow the continuous pounding of my feet and the acceleration of my heart rate helped ease my anxiety and introduced me to a part of myself that I had long denied: the Warrior. Running and consistent exercise helped me overcome the anorexia-bulimia, but in reality, it did so much more. It helped me to integrate my feminine side, which I had been using exclusively in childhood, with my masculine side. I learned to integrate the masculine and feminine first with athletics and then expanded that knowledge into other areas of my life.

As with most new things, I was awkward at first with this integration. At times in my twenties I leaned a little heavier on the masculine side, becoming tougher at work and a lean, mean running machine, competitive and driven, outside work. I would wake up early to run, go to work, then after work go out for another hard run, track workout, or to the gym to lift weights. I was exhilarated with the physicality of all of it. I felt alive and comfortable in my body for the first time and found myself quite addicted to that feeling.

It wasn't until I had children that I was able to break the intense addiction to running and allow the feminine to come back into my life. Children have a way of bringing out the best and worst in you and teaching you with so much love in between. I am grateful for each one of my children and understand now that they were the key to helping me integrate the masculine Warrior with the feminine Warrior part of me (see figure 1.6 in chapter 1). I learned to give and that being there for my children didn't mean I would die or go away.

I became mentally tougher and more resilient, more accepting, and less judgmental. Worries about beds being made and if I sent birthday cards out on time faded away. Also I gave up on those pre-children goals of: "I'll only feed my children organic, wholesome food," and "No child of mine will play with guns or watch TV for hours on end." I learned not to be so extreme with any views because they would come back to haunt me in the end. By my third child, I was sending him to preschool with Skittles in his lunch box as part of the "fruit group," and if I could get through a narrow, toy-strewn pathway to their beds at night to say prayers and kiss them good-night, I was happy.

My heroine's journey was that I found contentment within myself when I was true to myself and relaxed into that knowing. One can know that she is an Artisan or Warrior, but if through preconceived notions thinks that she "should" be somebody else, or at least act like somebody else, she may experience anxiety and discomfort.

The second part of my heroine's journey was to teach the message to have enough courage and faith to be who you really are. Although difficult, there are hundreds and thousands of women who are doing this every day. Some of them famous and some of them not. The world would be such a boring place if we didn't have our differences. How could the world function if we were all Kings? Who would do the work? What would happen if we were all Servers or Artisans? All aspects are essential to the "running" of our planet. The best thing we can do for others is to truly honor who we are. Then and only then will we be able to accept the similarities and differences in them.

Your story may be different than mine. The point is to take the time to reflect. Think back on your life. What have been your successes and failures? What has given you the most energy and when have you been the most proud?

A woman who explored her uniqueness in a different way was Cora Lee Johnson (Server-Priest-Scholar). Cora grew up picking cotton in the fields of Georgia. She also worked in a factory, was uneducated and poor—but she had a dream. Her dream was to some day have her own sewing center.

Married at fourteen, she had a difficult life and lost six babies because she worked so hard in the cotton fields. She cleaned homes, nursed her mother until she died, then her husband ran off with another woman. At sixty-two, injured in a car accident, she lost her job. At this point, a lot of people would have given up, but not Cora. Although defeated and feeling dejected, she began to attend community workshops and in her words, "saw things uneducated folks could do for their community if they really wanted." She didn't realize you could do so much with so little and she started to sew.

Nobody encouraged her. She talked about her dream to get more sewing machines so that others could learn to sew, too. People thought she was crazy. Eventually, someone listened and helped her get a grant from the Sapelo Foundation. With the money, she was able to create the Truetlen County Community Sewing Center and teach girls to sew.

She never turned anybody away because they couldn't pay to learn, because she wanted to teach the value of life. She used the time to talk to welfare mothers about learning to make their lives better so they didn't have to keep repeating the cycle of poverty and despair. Most importantly, she listened and made them feel as if they were people that deserved to be listened to. In time, she gathered her stories and took them to the United Nations World Summit on Social Development. She spoke about the struggle to obtain better housing and healthcare for the poor and has lobbied the Georgia Legislature and Congress on behalf of poor people. Cora Lee Johnson explored her own uniqueness and was able to use what she learned from personal hardship and observations to help empower and improve the quality of life for others.

What is your journey and what do you dream? Explore them by stopping to pause and reflect. Go inward to create your own personal vision.

Develop a Personal Life Vision

In order to know how to get somewhere, you must first know where you are going. This is easily accomplished by spending time to put together a few sentences that articulate your vision for your life. Your vision answers the questions: "Why am I here? What purpose do I have to fulfill for my time on the planet?"

Your vision could be something simple, such as providing for your family or bringing music to the world. Or your vision could be more complicated, such as one that involves teamwork. It could be to inspire other people or to provide the platform so that others can spread their wings. Whatever your vision, honor it and use it as a guide from which to measure how effectively you are leading your life.

An exercise that is used by Staub-Leadership Consultants during its High-Impact Leadership Seminar is effective in helping you create your vision. Allow yourself to have some quiet time and reflect on the following.

EXERCISE

Creating a Personal Vision[1]

Imagine you are on your deathbed. You have twenty minutes left to live, and you are reviewing your life. What does your life look like? What are you proud of? What are you disappointed in? How have you lived your life? What was the meaning of the life? What was your purpose in living the way you lived and doing the things you did? If you could go back and change any part of it, what would you change? Why? Look really hard at the values your life demonstrated. If you had to come up with an epitaph for this life, what would it be?

Now: How would you like to be living? What meaning would you like your life to have? If you could have a new lease on life and begin again, what would you choose as your guiding star? What are you really here to accomplish and to do? What vision do you have of the life you'd like to create? What is your sense of mission?

Pause for a moment and write down a brief statement of vision and mission for your life.

What would you like to have achieved, learned, experienced? Make a list. Be specific.

1._____

2._____

3._____

4._____

Look at yourself as you are today. What changes do you need to make to help you achieve your vision? Are you on track to get where you want to go?

_____

_____

_____

_____

Chapter Summary

Get to know your inner self by directing your energy inward.

➤ Honor your journey.

➤ Relax.

➤ Spend quiet time in reflection or meditation daily.

➤ Listen. Pay attention to your thoughts and intuitions.

➤ Journal. Write down your thoughts and dreams. Use writing to deal with difficult situations.

➤ Give yourself feedback. How do you feel? More centered? Powerful? Self-assured? What things are working for you? What things aren't? Make a note of both. It will help you take care of yourself.

➤ Explore your uniqueness.

➤ Create a personal vision. Decide what you want to do. Where you want to go. Who you want to be for the next three months, then a year, then long-term. Look at where you spend your time. Evaluate if you are spending time on things that will help you realize your vision. If not, why aren't you? If so, encourage yourself to stay centered and focused.

The Way We're Going

Hear that storm dancing on the river
Shower over me
Rain feels so forgiving
The sky's a canopy
I'm this lonely swimmer leaving part of me
Ripples in the water rolling out to sea
All I know is folding in together
Colors on a run
Fade away forever
The circle's never done
I'm just barely breathing
Face up in the rain
I give into the living,
We seldom know...
The way we're going
The seeds we're holding
Let them scatter where they will
There's a dream that's growing
A leaf unfolding
Give it heart and make it real
Far away a world we don't remember
Awaken one by one
All of us together can sparkle in the sun
Then we'll become that river
Waters warm and clean
Precious earth forgive us
And then we'll know...

(Chorus)
But I know sometimes there is more in life
Is there something more we can do?
Let our love flow high and our spirits rise
Let our eyes stay wide shining new, ever new.
Hear that storm dancing on the river
Shower over me
Rain feels so forgiving
The sky's a canopy
I'm this lonely swimmer leaving part of me
Ripples in the water
But now I know
The way we're going
The seeds we're holding
Let them scatter where they will
There's a dream that's growing
A leaf unfolding
Give it heart and make it real.

MUSIC AND LYRICS BY MICHAEL TOMLINSON
Face Up In the Rain CD

"Courage has nothing to do with your determination to be great. It has to do with what you decide in that moment when you are called upon. No matter how small the moment, or how personal, it is a moment when your life takes a turn and the lives of those around you take a turn because of you."

RITA DOVE
Appointed U.S. Poet Laureate in 1993,
Rita Dove is the first black poet laureate and,
at age forty-one, the youngest. She won
a Pulitzer Prize in 1987 for Thomas and Beulah.

"Has my daring changed the world? No, but it changed the world of our family. Have I cured a disease? No, but I finally gave more than lip service to one of the true ills of humanity."

SUSAN WINSTON
Susan Winston is a television producer and founder
and president of Blank & Bodi Productions Los Ange-
les. Her quote was inspired by her recognition of the
need for adoption of girls in China.

CHAPTER THREE

COURAGE

THE JOURNEY OF THE HEROINE BEGINS WITH THE CALL TO ADVENTURE, and it takes courage to hear the call. It also takes courage to dream of what the adventure may bring and have the drive and great will to take action to realize it. Above all, it helps to have a goal, a guiding light, or vision to make sure you stay on the path. If not, you may become sidetracked and lose sight of why you started.

Anita Roddick (Priest) is a woman who had the courage to dream and to turn her dreams into reality. A passionate and energetic businesswoman, spokesperson, activist, and writer, she is the driving force behind The Body Shop, a multimillion-dollar business that was conceived of and created in her home. Anita began gathering herbal remedies and folklore from locals in Littlehampton, England, in 1976. In the beginning, she dreamed of creating a natural, environmentally conscious cosmetic store. She sold her products in small plastic recyclable bottles because she didn't have enough money to buy more containers. Little did she realize she would be at the forefront of the retail environmental movement.

As her business grew, she championed causes. She wanted to empower women through her business, not tell them they needed to buy her products to be beautiful. Her ads were hip and to the point, and expressed her belief that women were beautiful just the way they are. In her autobiography, *Body & Soul: Profits With Principles—The Amazing Success Story of Anita Roddick & The Body Shop*, she said, "I hate the beauty business. It is a monster industry selling unattainable dreams. It lies. It cheats. It exploits women."[1]

Not one to mince words, Anita and her husband Gordon went on to realize their dream along with her passion and desire to create social and environmental changes. In the U.S., to encourage voting, she used The Body Shop as voter registration sites. When she opened a store in Harlem, she turned the profits back into the community. She travels the world searching for ways to improve the quality of life. Whether it is in poverty-stricken Third World countries or in the poor deltas of the southern Mississippi in the U.S., Anita Roddick takes it to the people.

Today, The Body Shop has more than 1,700 stores in forty-seven countries with profits at $500 million. Yet Anita's favorite saying is, "If you think you are too small to have an impact, try going to bed with a mosquito. This little mosquito wakes up every morning thinking, "This is my last day'. I must jam everything into it. There's no time for mediocrity. This is no damned dress rehearsal!"[2]

Although, Anita Roddick's passion and courage have brought her great success, they also have led to trouble. She has made her mistakes along the way: bad business decisions, trusting the wrong people, and forcing her views when she needed to listen. Her strength has been her resiliency and willingness to change.

Another woman of courage with dreams of social and political change is Aung San Suu Kyi (pronounced aung-sahn-soo-chee), the figurehead of Burma's quest for freedom and a democratic government.

This fifty-year-old woman, greatly feared by the military regime in power in Burma (currently named Myanmar), was put under house arrest for six years and forbidden to leave the country to see her husband or two children if she ever wanted to return. Aung San Suu Kyi (Priest-King) is the daughter of the late Burmese national hero, General Aung San, who led the resistance movement that brought Burma its first taste of independence in 1948.

Educated abroad, she returned in 1988 to address a country in crisis, where students were being massacred protesting against the prevailing military regime. She bravely stood and spoke for democracy and freedom of expression in the face of a military standoff with Burmese students. The army unit was ordered to aim their rifles and fire, but an army major intervened and prevented her assassination.

Aung San Suu Kyi has had a tremendous influence over her people. In a videotaped speech smuggled out of Burma and given to the 1995 International Forum on Women in Beijing, she said:

> *"If to these universal benefits of the growing emancipation of women can be added the "peace dividend" for human development offered by the end of the Cold War, spending less on the war toys of grown men and much more on the urgent needs of humanity as a whole, then truly the next millennia will be an age the like of which has never been seen in human history. But there still remain many obstacles to be overcome before we can achieve this goal. And not least among those obstacles are intolerance and insecurity."[3]*

In 1991, she was awarded the Nobel Peace Prize while under house arrest for her part in promoting peace and democracy. She was released in 1995, but still fearing she would not be allowed to reenter the country if she left, she remains in Burma. Separated from her family since 1990, she was not even able to visit her husband before he died in 2000. During a 1996 interview by *Marie Claire* magazine, she was asked if she regretted not returning to England to be with her husband and sons. She replied that she believed it was her choice and not a sacrifice. She felt that her people had made greater sacrifices and that they were at greater risk.

She still believes that Burma will flourish again under a proper political and economic system. A French magazine published an article about her titled, "A Light in the Night," and when asked what she thought about it, she replied that she didn't like to be thought of as anything more than an ordinary person. "Women who have been taught that modesty and pliancy are among the prized virtues of our gender are marvelously equipped for the learning process," said Aung San Suu Kyi. "But they must be given the opportunity to turn these often merely passive virtues into positive assets for the society in which they live."[4]

Anita Roddick and Aung San Suu Kyi are women of passion, women of courage, women who work to realize their goals. Such women are all around us. They go inward to develop their vision and come back with the energy to bring that vision to others.

> **Life is a daring adventure or nothing at all.**
> HELEN KELLER

Going for the Goal

The goal is a primary motivation in life and underlies the desire or drive for completion. Aside from the aspect, it is the most important characteristic or overleaf of one's personality. The goal is what the aspect tries to achieve and is much like a personal vision for your life.

The aspects of your personality will seek to bring about situations that will allow you the opportunity to work towards your goal. You will feel connected and satisfied when you are acting from the positive pole of your goal. Conversely, you will feel disconnected and as if something is missing when you are acting from the negative pole of your goal, or putting your energy somewhere else.

For example, a King with the goal of acceptance may feel uncomfortable when she is in a powerful leadership position. She may discover that people betray and undermine her until she begins to be careful about who she allows to help her. By being more selective about how she goes about her position, she finds her job easier. Because she is able to achieve her goals, she is more willing to be gracious to those who betrayed her. She can look at them nonjudgmentally, even to the point of realizing how they helped her to learn acceptance. Acceptance does not mean to let caution go to the wind. It encourages you to accept others where they are, instead of demanding that they change in order for you to accept them.

Another example is growth. A Scholar with the goal of growth may feel reluctant to change. As the neutral aspect, she may prefer to read and stay unscathed by the roller coaster of emotions that comes with learning and growing, especially concerning relationships. If she withdraws or fights the change, she will become confused and feel cut off from what she needs to learn. If she opens to the learning, she will evolve and grow towards realizing her goal, which will be the most satisfying to the true essence of her being.

Each goal, as with the aspect, has a positive and negative pole. Achievement of the goal is easier and flows when a woman operates from the positive side. To get out of the negative pole, she may need to slide to the opposite goal on the axis and work in that area until she can get back on track.

A woman with the goal of growth who is changing so much she becomes scattered and confused may need to slide to re-evaluation and take time to sort things out in order to get back to the positive side of growth. A woman with the goal of dominance may find she is too controlling and will need to slide to the goal of submission to remember how to value people and how to invite people to participate instead of coercing them to do a task. Goals fall into one of seven general categories.[5] See figure 3.1.

FIGURE 3.1

The Seven Aspects Model: Goals

INSPIRATION GOALS		ACTION GOALS	
+Simplicity	+Evolution	+Devotion	+Leadership
Re-evaluation	**Growth**	**Submission**	**Dominance**
-Withdrawal	-Confusion	-Subservience	-Dictatorship
EXPRESSIVE GOALS		ASSIMILATION GOALS	
+Sophistication	+Unconditional love	+Free flowing	
Discrimination	**Acceptance**	**Relaxation**	
-Rejection	-Ingratiation	-Inertia	

FIGURE 3.2

Percentages in the Population[6]

Re-evaluation	1%	Growth	40%
Discrimination	2%	Acceptance	30%
Submission	10%	Dominance	10%
Relaxation	7%		

> **INSPIRATION GOALS**
> Re-evaluation ——————— Growth

Re-evaluation

This goal is only selected by a small percentage of the population. It is introspective and usually relates to the integration internally of many experiences. Sometimes a temporary experience of re-evaluation can come about by drug use. These people may slide into silence, withdraw from the world, and look at the people and things around them from a simplistic point of view.

Due to the nature of this goal, few individuals have re-evaluation as their key goal. The positive side of re-evaluation is simplicity. The acting and believing that life is simple and uncomplicated. There is a sense of awe and wonder about someone with this goal. The negative pole shows itself as withdrawal, as being internalized, spaced-out, or regressed.

Famous people with the goal of re-evaluation: Buddha, Albert Einstein, James Joyce, Helen Keller, Jean-Paul Sartre, George Schultz, and Neil Young.[7]

Growth

The goal of growth is in some ways the opposite of re-evaluation. To be in growth means change and fluctuation. Growth is usually seen as a lifetime of tremendous activity and one of new experiences. It may also seem that a person with a goal of growth physically changes her appearance many times during her lifetime. It has been said that the appearance of some women changes so dramatically that they actually look like different people. Growth is a popular goal; approximately 40 percent of the population chooses growth as a goal. As a result, 40 percent of the earth's population is experiencing growth as a goal all at once, which may explain why there appears to be so much change going on.

A person with the goal of growth doesn't expect that the growth has to be fun. Sometimes a woman working through this goal creates challenges for herself that are painful. She may find that what she has been doing actually leads to nowhere. If a woman with the goal of growth believes that she needs to read ten novels in a month or hike all the 14,000-foot mountains in Colorado, she will do it. Some women, to their dismay, find that after they complete a task, it really didn't get them to their goal after all. After a period of "re-evaluation," they are able to create a new vision and find new tasks that will help them achieve what they wish to accomplish.

One telling characteristic of the goal of growth is the need to talk about experiences and what they mean. Women in growth tend to be self-oriented and focused on resolving inner conflicts. It is important to allow women who are experiencing grwoth the space and time to work through their issues. The negative side of growth is confusion, self-absorption, driven, complicated, and being ignorant of the needs of others. The positive side of the goal of growth is to be evolving, clear, progressive, willing to take on challenges, and have the ability to be clear about purpose.

Famous people with the goal of growth are: Kirstie Alley, Lynn Andrews, Lucille Ball, Kim Basinger, Ken Burns, Carlos Casteneda, Kevin Costner, Robert Downey Jr., Patty Duke, Bridget Fonda, Betty Ford, Mel Gibson, Jesse Jackson, Jacqueline Kennedy Onassis, Shirley MacLaine, John Lennon, Steve Martin, Paul Newman, Yoko Ono, Faith Popcorn, Eleanor Roosevelt, Susan Sarandon, Gail Sheehy, Gloria Steinem, Barbara Walters, and Oprah Winfrey.[8]

EXPRESSIVE GOALS
Discrimination ——————— Acceptance

Discrimination

The goal of discrimination is chosen by only 2 percent of the population. The aim of this difficult goal is to develop the skill of discernment in order to weed out experiences, people, or things that are unwanted. Discrimination helps one to focus only on what is important and what or who will help you achieve your goal.

The positive pole of discrimination is sophistication, refinement, discernment, and well-developed critical faculties. A woman operating out of the positive side of this goal would be particular about the kind of clothes she wore, or her friends. She may use her sophisticated taste and ability to discern to be a literary critic or wine reviewer and will feel most fulfilled when being rewarded for her discriminating nature.

The negative pole of discrimination can look like prejudice and being overly opinionated, snobbish, and quick to judge self and others. A woman in this state can appear difficult and judgmental, which can in turn cause her to be rejected by others. This rejection reinforces the tendency to reject and perpetuates a vicious cycle. To overcome this cycle of rejection, it helps if the woman seeks to understand the source of her own prejudices. It is also important for the woman to take a wider view of the situation or to "draw the larger circle." In fact, the best way for her to break the rejection cycle is to start with (unconditionally) loving herself. She will need to do this for herself before she tries to do it with others. As with the stumbling blocks of arrogance and self-deprecation, the rejection cycle or negative side of discrimination, is fueled by low self-esteem. Low self-esteem withers in the face of unconditional love. Confidence and self-esteem grow when a woman believes in herself and is able to see the current reality of a situation without judging herself or others.

Famous people with the goal of discrimination are: Jacqueline Bisset, Tom Brokaw, William F. Buckley, Michael Caine, Marcia Clark, Julia Child, Glenn Close, Joan Collins, Katie Couric, Willem Dafoe, Isadora Duncan, Kirsten Dunst, Ralph Fiennes, Richard Gere, John Heard, Anthony Hopkins, Linda Hunt, Elizabeth Hurley, Iman, Peter Jennings, Val Kilmer, Jessica Lange, John McEnroe, Julianne Moore, Leonard Nimoy, Jane Pauley, Emily Post, Prince, Keanu Reeves, Joan Rivers, Cokie Roberts, and Cybill Shepard.[9]

Acceptance

About a third of the population chooses the goal of acceptance. Women with this goal tend to accept whatever occurs in their lives. Being accepted is important to them, so they tend to be people-pleasers and to be agreeable. These women have a hard time saying "no" and find it difficult to assert themselves. They may find themselves stuck with an unwanted or untenable situation merely because they didn't want to make waves. They may find that people take advantage of them and misuse them because of an underlying fear of rejection.

To get out of this inability to assert themselves, women with the goal of acceptance will find that they need to be more discriminating and fastidious about their time. In doing so, they have slid from the negative pole of acceptance to the positive pole of discrimination all along the Expressive Axis.

Famous people with the goal of acceptance: Paula Abdul, Angela Bassett, Candice Bergen, Robert Bly, Jeff and Lloyd Bridges, Christie Brinkley, Pierce Brosnan, Sandra Bullock, Joseph Campbell, Joan Cusack, Ram Dass, Catherine Deneuve, Olympia Dukakis, Wayne Dyer, Kathie Lee Gifford, Whoopi Goldberg, Hugh Grant, Melanie Griffith, Scott Hamilton, Audrey Hepburn, Billie Holliday, Whitney Houston, Magic Johnson, Carl Jung, Diane Keaton, Ricki Lake, Dalai Lama, Ann Landers, Courtney Love, Van Morrison, Julia Ormond, Sarah Jessica Parker, Roseanne, RuPaul, Carly Simon, Meryl Streep, Jessica Tandy, James Taylor, and Abigail Van Buren.[10]

ACTION GOALS
Submission ——————— Dominance

Submission

This goal makes up 10 percent of the population at any given time. It is the act of placing oneself in the service of a cause or a person and involves putting others' needs before your own. Many times women with the goal of submission look for a teacher and seek life in a religious order, such as a convent. They may also devote themselves to a cause, such as Mother Teresa with the starving children of India, or they devote their lives to research in the name of saving a species of animals, such as Jane Goodall, who worked tirelessly to save chimpanzees, or Dian Fossey, who devoted her life to preserve gorillas in Africa.

The positive side of submission can be seen in an individual who lives a life that brings her satisfaction through devotion. Examples could be: raising a large family, commitment to marriage, or devotion to a career or spiritual cause. Women with a goal of submission may also dedicate themselves to the arts or the study of science in a devoted way.

The negative side of submission can be seen when a woman allows herself to be victimized, brutalized, subservient, or helpless. She can get out of this bondage and poor role by taking on the powerful characteristics of the opposite goal of the Action Axis, that of dominance. For example, a battered woman who lives in fear of her life can take charge by using personal leadership skills to guide her. She can set a vision of what she wants her life to be like, develop a strategy to achieve her goal, and then set her plan in to action by building a support group. Once she comes from a place of dominance as opposed to being the victim in submission she can set herself free and find a more positive place on which to place her goal of devotion.

Famous people with the goal of submission are: Joan Baez, John Bradshaw, Eric Clapton, Tom Cruise, Robert Dole, Clarissa Pinkola Estes, Jane Fonda, Dian Fossey, Princess Diana, Thich Nhat Hanh, Joan of Arc, Mr. Rogers, Mia Farrow, Mahatma Gandhi, Chief Joseph, Martin Luther King Jr., Lao Tsu, Florence Nightingale, Nancy Reagan, and Christopher Reeve.[11]

Dominance

This goal is the complement of submission on the Action Axis. As such, people will experience the most success with this goal when they take an active leadership role. Women with the goal of dominance will tend to rise to the top of any situation. They may reach leadership positions at work or within their families, communities, or organizations. They possess an innate drive to be in control. Some people may experience this as bossiness, but these women must lead in order to feel fulfilled. Their learning comes in how they lead, not what they do.

The current social, political, and business environment provides ample opportunities for women to lead. This has not historically been the case, and women with a goal for dominance or with the King, Priest, or Storyteller Aspects have found it difficult to feel fulfilled within the confines of limited roles.

The positive side of dominance shows as a leader who is authoritative, determined, outgoing, and operates towards a win-win situation. The negative side of dominance is found with a leader who is dictatorial, demanding, pushy, overwhelming, controlling, and domineering. Women stuck in the negative pole of dominance can get out of it by sliding to the positive pole of submission, which is devotion. They must learn to surrender. Once they devote themselves to the demands of the situation, they can then lead appropriately.

Famous people with the goal of dominance are: Maya Angelou, Sandra Bernhard, Bono (from U2), Barbara Boxer, Jane Brody, Diahann Carroll, Fidel Castro, Catherine the Great, Coco Chanel, Connie Chung, Cleopatra, Hillary Clinton, Robert DeNiro, Elizabeth Dole, Fran Drescher, Chris Evert, Jodie Foster, Indira Ghandi, Mikhail and Raisa Gorbachev, Alan Greenspan, Gene Hackman, Don Henley, Chrissie Hynde, Don Johnson, Grace Jones, Jack Kevorkian, Genghis Khan, Madonna, Imelda Marcos, Demi Moore, Martina Navritalova, Sandra Day O'Connor, Sean Penn, Mary Lou Retton, Phyllis Schafly, Sharon Stone, Margaret Thatcher, Bruce Willis, and Katarina Witt.[12]

> **ASSIMILATION GOAL**
> Relaxation

Relaxation

The seventh goal has no pair and is the neutral goal. Approximately, 7 percent of the population is in the relaxation goal at any one time, and it is considered a lifetime of rest. The goal of relaxation is to let life flow easily and effortlessly. Some people spend most of their life fighting this and may take a long time to "relax" into their goal. Their lives tend to unfold without intense drama or effort on their part. They are often born into wealth or possess talents and skills which allow them to be well-paid and respected. Things tend to come to them quite easily. These women are often envied by others, especially other women.

In the positive, relaxation is free-flowing, unstressed, easygoing, and fun-loving. In the negative, relaxation is lazy, uncommitted, and stagnant. Women in the negative pole struggle more than is necessary. They can get out of this stuck place by letting life flow and using breathing exercises such as in yoga, Qui Gong, or Pilates. They must practice letting life be and stepping out of the way as in the martial arts.

Famous people with the goal of relaxation are: Antonio Banderas, Sheryl Crow, Andy Garcia, Hugh Hefner, Mariel Hemingway, Georgia O'Keefe, Brad Pitt, Claudia Schiffer, and William Shatner.[13]

> **EXERCISE**

Discover Your Goal [14]

To decide which goal is yours, take the following quiz. Read the alternatives below and see if you can identify the one that motivates you most.

1. If things aren't going my way, I fear I'm losing. Life is a competition. I always want to win, no matter what.

2. More than anything else, I want to be dedicated to someone or something. I'm most comfortable when I feel devoted. I put others ahead of myself regularly.

3. More than anything I want people to like me. I hate being rejected. If someone spreads unkind rumors about me, I would be deeply wounded and find it difficult to confront him or her.

4. I don't enjoy things unless they are exactly right. I am picky about who my friends are, what I wear, and what I do. I am critical, and I find others highly critical of me.

5. I like to be constantly learning, experiencing things, and changing. Just when I think I've mastered something, I feel compelled to learn something else, to start something new. Sometimes I become overwhelmed at the enormity of what I am doing and have to pull back to sort things out.

6. My life seems to revolve around one theme. My experiences reinforce that theme over and over again. Much of what I experience is affected by my physical condition and I am severely limited in my ability to get around.

7. I don't feel ambitious or driven to accomplish anything major in my life. I seem to ride effortlessly from one thing to another. Life is pleasant.

Key: *Find the corresponding number of the sentence you selected. That is your goal.*

1. Dominance   5. Growth
2. Submission   6. Re-evaluation
3. Acceptance   7. Relaxation
4. Discrimination

Choosing a Life Task

In addition to a goal, each person chooses a life task, which can be complemented by the goal. For example, if your goal is growth, you will continually be in situations that force you to take a look at yourself and learn from them. These situations may be uncomfortable, which creates the impetus for change. The discomfort propels you to find a better way.

You could then use the information gathered from these growth experiences to write a book to teach others about learning and growing. Your goal is growth, but your life task is to teach and inspire large groups of people through writing.

It is not a simple process to figure out your life task. One exercise to help you gain clarity is looking at what you enjoy doing. Ask yourself what energizes you. Where and what are you doing when you are the happiest?

You may not be able to figure out your life task until later in life. For most women, a life task becomes apparent by the age of forty-two. By the time we reach the age of forty-two, we have probably well-established our identity and are freer to do our life task work. Most of your life up until that point is spent working on relationships and sorting out who you will become. When you begin to realize your life task, you will know intuitively that it is right. The awareness starts deep inside and is related to that "internal homing device" that guides you towards wholeness or completeness.

Seven is an important number in our development throughout our lifetime. Every seven years, we have an opportunity to recreate ourselves. This happens physically in that we have new cell growth that replaces the old, but it also occurs in our nonphysical body, in that we face different decisions and rites of passage. These decision points tend to follow a cyclical pattern of seven years.

Around the age of seven, we begin to individuate and develop the strongest part of our personality, the part that we primarily present to the world. In terms of the Seven Aspects Model, it is the Primary Aspect. Other theories of psychological development corroborate this time frame.

According to W. Harold Grant, a noted contributor to Myers-Briggs Personality writings and an expert in Jungian typology, the type development is a process that tends to grow with chronological age. In his book *From Image to Likeness*, Grant makes it easier for someone to determine his or her true type by showing how one particular mental function is stronger or developed over time. This ground breaking theory applies to the Seven Aspects Model and is explained as follows:

Grant's Theory of Type Development indicates that from:

Ages 6–12 The Dominant mental function (Primary Aspect) is developed. Year 7 falls into this category.

Ages 13–20 Auxiliary mental function (Secondary Aspect) is developed. Year 14 falls into this category.

Ages 21–35 Tertiary mental function (Tertiary Aspect) is developed. Years 21, 28, and 35 fall into this category.

Ages 36–50 Inferior mental function (Goal) is developed. Years 42 and above fall into this category.

The Seven Aspects Model develops as follows:

Ages	*Development*
7	Primary Aspect
14	Secondary Aspect (Complementary aspect)
21–35	Tertiary Aspect (Family aspect)
21–42	Life task apparent. Goals evident. A look at the personal history of dealing with problems reveals how stumbling blocks were instrumental in helping to achieve personal goals and work towards life task.

EXERCISE

Assessing Life Task and Goal

Find a quiet place to relax. Have a pad of paper handy. Let go of all of your cares and worries. Take "should" and "have to" out of your mind. This is your time and space **to be.**

Breathe slowly and deeply. Believe that inside yourself, you have the answers. Pray that you will be guided to hear and see them.

Imagine that you no longer exist; you have simply vanished. Imagine what people would say about you.

How would they remember you?

What would you like them to remember about what you have contributed to their lives?

How do you feel?

Is there unfinished business?

Did you leave dissatisfied that you did not finish what you came to accomplish?

Note your responses to these questions. Is there a common theme? Make note of this.

After reflecting on your responses, write down some ideas of what your life task might be. Keep in mind what energizes you. That will give you a good idea of where to start.

Think about what you selected as your goal in the "Exercise: Discover Your Goal."

Think about what you are doing when you are the happiest and feeling the most fulfilled.

Are you happiest and feeling fulfilled when:
- Things are changing (Growth).
- You feel free-flowing and floating (Relaxation).
- You are in the leadership position (Dominance).
- You are being devoted and in service (Submission).

- You feel nonjudgmental in unconditional love (Acceptance).
- Things are refined and sophisticated (Discrimination).
- Life is simple (Re-evaluation).

   Continue to think about what you do that energizes you the most. Using all of this information, what do you feel your purpose is? Write this as your life task.

   _____

Goals Change Over Time

Your goals may change over time. If you are close to the age of forty-two or older, you have had enough life experience to discern your task and goals. If you need further help, read the section on personal vision in chapter 2. Other information on developing a personal vision or discovering your life task may be found at http://www.commonboundaries.com. The Myers-Briggs Type Indicator and Enneagram are two other personality models to help uncover your type and life task.

   Although there are numerous books to help you on this path of discovering, it is most important that you spend time with yourself. Look inside for answers. Seek to understand yourself first and use all forms of teachings as information. In the end, you are the only person who can say if the information applies to you. You are the only person who can articulate your life task. Only you know.

   One interesting way to look at the purpose of life task is to see it in terms of coming from your heart rather than your mind. Catherine Ryan Hyde illustrated the idea of purpose or life task in her book *Pay It Forward*, which was made into a movie. In the book, Trevor, a twelve-year-old boy faced with an assignment given by his junior high teacher, comes up with the idea of "paying it forward" instead of paying someone back when they do something for you of value. It requires that you "pay it forward" to three people and that the gift must be something significant that the person really wants or needs. It involves getting to know the person or situation enough to determine what gift is really needed.

   The book shows the fear and stumbling blocks that arise in the face of change and the human aspect of how we deal with it all. Trevor is successful in starting the "Pay It Forward" trend, but becomes discouraged because it doesn't look like what he thought it would or because it takes longer than he expected. In the end, he became aware that he had touched many lives with his idea, but was mostly satisfied because he had accomplished his personal goal. Trevor's life task was to dream and to create a radical new social idea. His goal was to learn unconditional love and acceptance. He accomplished this by forgiving his mother, and learning to love unconditionally. In this way, his goal and life task complemented each other, both were essential in helping him achieve success.

Some Books to Help You On the Path of Discovery

The Unfolding Self: Psychosynthesis and Counseling by Molly Brown

Discovering Your Soul's Purpose by Mark Thurston

Illusions: The Adventures of a Reluctant Messiah by Richard Bach

One Day My Soul Just Opened Up by Iyanla Vanzant

Awakening the Heroes Within: Twelve Archetypes to Help Us Find Ourselves and Transform Our World by Carol Pearson

Please Understand Me by David Kiersey and Marilyn Bates

Integrity in Depth by John Beebe

Do What You Are: Discover the Perfect Career for You Through the Secrets of Personality Type by Barbara Barron-Tieger & Paul Tieger

Awakening Intuition by Frances Vaughn

Who Am I? Personality Types for Self-Discovery by Robert Forager

> ### Facing the Challenge
>
> Why is it important to know our goal and life task? Because we can use this information to face challenges. Robert (Dusty) E. Staub II wrote a book titled *The Seven Acts of Courage,* which offers stories and practical exercises illustrating the courageous acts we take in our daily and professional lives. Some of these acts have been included in this chapter to further illustrate the idea of the courage needed to overcome the stumbling blocks in order to achieve our goals. Staub's Seven Acts of Courage are:
>
> 1. The courage to dream and put forth that dream.
> 2. The courage to see current reality.
> 3. The courage to confront.
> 4. The courage to be confronted.
> 5. The courage to learn and grow.
> 6. The courage to be vulnerable, to love.
> 7. The courage to act.[15]

Seeing Things Clearly

Aung San Suu Kyi, Anita Roddick, along with hundred of thousands of women show courage in their daily lives. Rosa Parks showed courage when she refused to move to the back of the bus. Cora Lee Johnson showed courage when she didn't give up even when life kept beating her down. Women who are brave enough to see things clearly have the courage to see current reality. It isn't sugarcoated.

They get past distortions or tricks that our minds play in order to protect us from pain. These false perceptions steer us away from the reality of the situation and leave us stuck with our assumptions and beliefs. Like the ostrich, we think that if we don't see it, then we don't have to acknowledge it. But the reality is that everyone around us does see what we don't wish to see and that makes for greater pain and failure in the long run. Staub's book refers to four defense systems we turn to in order to mask reality.[16] They are:

➤ Denial

➤ Repression

➤ Projection and distortion

➤ Rationalization

Denial is when we turn away from what is right in front of our faces. It is being blinded to whatever contradicts our sense of reality, and not being open enough to accept another viewpoint. It is limiting and blocks growth.

Repression is when we stuff down emotions or awarenesses instead of letting them come to the surface. It is analogous to someone who is trying to hold balls under water. As the person frantically tries to control one group of balls, others pop up. It is nearly impossible to keep the old ones submerged while new ones keep surfacing. It is a losing proposition and takes a lot of time and energy. Repression is a defense that we use to block out painful experiences and memories.

Projection and distortion are defensive mechanisms that enable us to reshape what we see. We explain what is happening out of our preconceived assumptions and beliefs. Distortion is when we see our fears, expectations, doubts, and beliefs instead of the reality in front of us.

Rationalization is a defense mechanism that enables us to explain away anything that does not meet with our view of the situation at hand. It also enables us to justify doing something we know is wrong but we want to do anyway. Rationalization gives us peace over our internal struggles. It helps us overcome cognitive dissonance.

An excellent exercise to overcome these defense mechanisms and to learn to see the current reality is to start with the resolution that you will be more aware of the world around you. Begin to take notice of how you affect other people and how they are affected by you. Pay attention to times when the four defense mechanisms come into play.

Sarah, a Storyteller-Scholar-Priest with the goal of growth, was shocked when her friend Rebecca confronted her. Rebecca told Sarah that she was inconsiderate and told jokes at other people's expense. Sarah countered that all her stories were in fun and that nobody took her seriously. Rebecca pointed out several instances in which friends were hurt by one of Sarah's stories. Sarah began to tear apart Rebecca's examples by saying "Oh, I didn't tell that story about Janet; you have it wrong. I told another story about her." And "You've got the facts wrong. I didn't say she was wearing a red dress. I said she was wearing a blue one."

Frustrated, Rebecca became angry and said, "You're missing the point! You hurt people when you poke fun at them. Even if you think it is funny, they certainly do not!"

Sarah looked at her and replied, "I don't know why you are getting so upset. It is not a big deal and as far as I can see, none of your business either. If so and so is angry about my stories, why doesn't she come and talk to me about it?"

Rebecca was flabbergasted that Sarah wasn't responding to what she had originally said. She walked away in resignation, dismayed that Sarah was closed to what she was saying. Sarah was in denial. She also projected her feelings onto Rebecca and distorted her point of view. As a Storyteller, Sarah may use people to get a laugh and rationalized that it was all in good fun. Rebecca's best hope would be to get Sarah to see how it feels from the point of view of the people about whom she is telling the story. Empathy for the other people will help her break free from her defense mechanisms. To get to that point, Sarah will need to develop the courage to be confronted in order to see current reality.

Ways to See Current Reality[17]

➤ Start by noticing what you most resist and end up arguing about. Entertain the possibility that you are defending yourself against deeper awareness. Take the viewpoint you most resist and explore it for any truth contained within it.

➤ Ask someone you trust to help you take a detailed and honest look at how you act, react, and impact others, and how you come across when dealing with others.

➤ Periodically, ask key people in your life, both personally and professionally, to give you feedback. Ask each: "What are my strengths? What am I doing that I should continue doing? What should I stop doing and why? What should I start doing?"

Listening to Feedback

Courage to be confronted goes hand in hand with the courage to see current reality. Anita Roddick found this out when she made some bad business decisions expanding into the U.S. and was forced to lay off employees. The reality of losing money came right up against her idealist views of taking care of her employees as if they were family. Her causes cost money, and in the long run, she was forced to make difficult business decisions. Anita grew through the process because she was willing to face reality and learn. She cut back on expenses, closed some stores, and let some employees go in order to turn her business around. She didn't have an easy time hearing the bad news, but she came through it and The Body Shop is thriving more than ever experiencing an 18 percent increase in sales for the first fiscal quarter of 2001.

If Anita had turned her back on the advice of accountants, investment analysts, and management consultants, The Body Shop might not be thriving. If she had said that she wouldn't close the stores, cut back on expenses, and fire employees, more people would have suffered. She learned from that experience and writes about it in her book, *Business As Unusual.*

Your ability to learn from criticism and confrontation depends on your capacity to embrace confrontation instead of relying on automatic defenses. This requires that you understand that to be in a relationship is to face regular criticism and confrontation. This is part of the nature of "relating."

Develop the Courage to Be Confronted[18]

1. Develop a support network to help you respond to criticism and confrontation without resorting to your automatic defenses. Whenever you do resort to your automatic defenses, have people around you who can compassionately help and encourage you to open up.

2. Give up the need to be "right." This means you must develop your self-esteem and inner wisdom to the point where you know it is more important to learn to relate to others, than to be "right."

3. Realize that the criticism that hooks you the most may be a red flag for you to take a closer look at what is going on inside. What are your thoughts and feelings?

In other words, instead of reacting, seek to understand. The point of this book is to look inside first to understand what you are thinking and feeling in order to be more effective in dealing with others.

Women with the goals of growth, acceptance, and submission will find it easier to be confronted than women with other goals. One of the key elements in successfully giving and receiving feedback is how someone is confronted. It is important to have the right tone and words. The most effective confrontation is when it is respectful. Regardless of someone's aspect or goal, she is able to listen and receive feedback much better when approached respectfully.

EXERCISE

*Resolve to Learn from Others
When They Criticize or Confront You*

To do this exercise:

1. **Protect yourself.** A prayer for protection is "I am surrounded in a bubble of protective white light. I cannot be harmed by anything that comes in. The feedback will be transformed into learning for my highest good."

2. **Open to the feedback.** Feel safe enough to embrace what is being said before you embrace it. Open and listen to the feedback. It is important to remember when receiving or giving feedback, that the feedback tells 100 percent about the person giving the feedback and 50 percent about the person receiving it. Therefore, just because someone says you talk too much, it doesn't necessarily mean that you talk too much. It just means that the person giving you the feedback perceives you as talking too much and that it gets in the way of your communication with each other.

3. **Create a support base.** Make a point to create a network of relationships in which those around you are supportive, compassionate, and honest enough to help you "see" when you are trapped in automatic, preprogrammed thinking, acting, and dealing with others.

Your support base: _____

_____

_____

_____

_____

_____

Learning and Growing

The courage to learn and grow involves giving up the need to be right. It feels as if you are moving from comfort and security to more uncomfortable ground because it throws you off balance and forces you to find a new point of equilibrium. Eventually, it drives you to let go of the known and find a new way of interacting with the world.

Practicing the courage to learn and grow is "essentially the courage to go beyond the first impulse that comes to you when you are challenged or in doubt or fear. It requires the willingness to face the unknown and the untried. It requires looking deep into your heart and soul, and letting go of the need to be right and to stay in control. It is found when we step into ambiguity and explore the unknown."[19] This practice involves stepping into "the abyss." Once you jump off into the unknown, there is no turning back; you are forever changed and in this way will also change the world around you.

By permission of Johnny Hart and Creators Syndicate, Inc.

Staub's book highlights material by Chris Argyriss, which explains how smart people stop learning because of their successful achievements. Argyriss goes on to emphasize that some people get stuck in being "right," and remain heavily vested in the dead weight of what worked for them in the past. "His studies show that we get stuck in behaviors that we believe contributed to our success," Staub writes. "We become attached to, even rigid about, particular ways of thinking, acting, and interacting. This may be fine if the old patterns continue to fit and serve the changing world, and continue to work effectively with new processes, relationships, or roles. But when they don't, which is often the case, we experience loss and failure, often blaming others while we hold tightly to our cherished beliefs and behaviors.[20]

Even the most well-meaning person can be blinded by tunnel vision caused by her need to be right.

The Courage to Learn and Grow [21]

1. Choose to learn in the moment.
2. Be curious, looking beneath the surface for the deeper impulse.
3. Let go of what you know.
4. Let go of "being right."
5. Get uncomfortable.
6. Listen with an open heart.
7. Reframe what you learn in a positive statement.
8. Always affirm yourself, even when you've done something wrong. Remember that growing and learning means making mistakes. Allow yourself the room to make them. Pat yourself on the back when you succeed.
9. Remember to affirm others when they succeed.

Motivations of Courage

Courage is situational and can mean different things to different people. *Webster's Collegiate Dictionary 2000* defines courage as the quality of mind or temperament that enables one to stand fast in the face of opposition, hardship, or danger. Courage is synonymous with boldness, fearlessness, heroism, backbone, determination, and persistence. Courage means having the heart to face challenges, and the will to see those challenges through. It is personified by someone who dares to break conventional boundaries and does it with integrity driven by an insatiable need to discover what lies beyond the horizon. It is also seen in one who dares to stand in the face of conflict or adversity to promote what she believes is right.

It is evidenced by the child who speaks out against the unfairness of the "in group" when group members are making fun of another child. It is in the face of the woman with cerebral palsy who shows courage by triumphing over her disability so that she can ski. It is apparent in the woman who stands up to peers and management at work to say, "My life is my own. I don't want to give twenty-four hours a day to my job. I need balance in my life, and I need to spend more time with my family."

When we think of courage, most of us think of larger than life heroic acts we hear about on TV or in the movies. "Man dives into river to save drowning child!" "Woman donates kidney to a woman she barely knows!" "Two climbers risk their lives saving skiers buried in an avalanche!" All extraordinary stories. All heroic. All courageous.

What about a different set of headlines: "Woman quits work to become a stay-at-home mom." She faces her deepest fear of losing her identity between diaper changes, endless cleaning, and the total giving that accompanies full-time motherhood. Or "Woman commits to working out the problems within her marriage instead of running away from them." Or "Daughter stands up for herself by saying, 'Mother, I don't like it when you try to control my life' even if it means being cut off from financial support."

These everyday occurrences also show courage. They are the types of courage that we use and show in our daily lives and are no less important than the more publicized courageous actions. Therefore, it is possible to look at courage as having two motivators:

1. Going from the inside out.

2. Coming from the outside and looking inward.

Outwardly directed courage will result in a brave act for the benefit of someone else. Inwardly directed courage will involve dealing with one's inner fear to overcome an emotional or psychological block.

Overcoming Fear

Personal acts of courage are often spurred by fear. Fear grips us, and it can paralyze and make us afraid of failure and success. It can be felt in our bodies as clammy hands, shaking muscles, heart palpitations, and a queasy stomach. It can make us cold and overcome us so much that we freeze. It can also cause adrenaline to flow so rapidly through our bloodstream that we become aggressive or resort to extreme measures to avoid it. Yet fear and the adrenaline that comes with it can also spur us on to be bigger than ourselves. It can compel us to confront when we've never done so. It can help us face the truth. It can help us leap off burning buildings, if need be. It can help us become heroes in our everyday lives.

Learning to overcome fear is a process that must be lived through experience and not through reading or intellectualizing. It cannot be imagined or wished away. One must live through it or "be engaged." As in the words of the famous French existentialist philosopher, Jean-Paul Sartre, "One must live in a state of engagement (l'engagement) to learn by getting one's hands dirty (les salles mains)."

Breathe and Let Go

There are numerous techniques to work through fear, and most involve breathing. Holding the breath constricts the muscles and adds to the tension brought about by fear. This tension is what causes the muscles to lock and continues the cycles of paralysis or inability to move and breathe.

The simple act of breathing helps calm the muscles and mind. As the thoughts that cause fear play through one's mind in an endless loop, one must learn to let them go. Treat the thoughts as if they were a screen saver on the computer. Watch them as they float by. Allow them to leave instead of energizing them with worry. You don't worry about the images on your screen saver, do you? Treat those continuous thoughts the same way. Breathing and using mental imagery is helpful. Holding positive images and thoughts in one's mind is also helpful.

Perform Mental Rehearsals

Part of overcoming fear is mental gymnastics. It is practicing techniques over and over again until they become second nature—until the time comes when they must be deliberate. One must go through calming techniques step by step. And in time, the anxiety produced by the fear will lessen. It is much like practicing a tennis stroke over and over until muscle memory takes over and you no longer have to say to yourself, "Okay, racquet back. Look at the ball. Follow through."

Meditate

In addition to breathing, some people find it helpful to meditate. Find a quiet place to pray, or practice breathing techniques to calm the mind and then draw upon this sense of peace when you are confronted with anxiety-producing situations.

Visualize and Journal

Other fear-fighting techniques are visualization and journaling. It is helpful to visualize yourself in a calm place and then in your mind invoke a situation that would normally cause fear. Using calming techniques gradually teaches you to associate the fearful situation with a sense of peacefulness instead of anxiety. Writing one's feelings about a fearful situation can also serve to alleviate the stress brought about by fear. It can be cathartic to release one's feelings on paper, which can give one insight into why certain situations provoke fear.

Face It

Another means of overcoming fear is simply to experience the situation head on and to keep doing it until the fear is mastered. It is much like the "whenever I feel afraid, I whistle a happy tune" philosophy from *The King and I*. Trick your fear. Watch your body language. Don't let the head drop or the panic overwhelm your body. Simply look fear in the eye and say, "I'm ready. Give it your best shot." The learning comes in putting on the trappings of being courageous even if you don't feel that way inside. Eventually, you will have an experience that proves you can do whatever you are afraid of doing. It is a way of pre-conditioning yourself to be courageous.

> **_Tips for Overcoming Fear_**
> 1. Breathe.
> 2. Go through mental rehearsals.
> 3. Meditate.
> 4. Write/journal.
> 5. Face it.

Facing Fear

One simple illustration of how facing fear has worked for me has been through tennis. In the beginning, I was emotional on the court. In frustration, I reprimanded myself, "Debbie, how could you do that?" I appeared down and dejected when I made a bad shot or double-faulted. Sure enough, when my opponents read my body language, they knew they had already won. The errors would snowball, and my frustrations and fears became a self-fulfilling prophecy: I would lose.

Over time, through help with an insightful coach, I learned to mask most of these frustrations and fears by improving my body language on court. I'm still not sure if it worked because my opponents were psyched-out by my confident demeanor or if I tricked myself into being what I really wanted to be: confident and fearless. All I know is that many times when I was down and in danger of losing the match or having a bad day, I would pull my chin up and look my opponent coolly in the eye. Nine times out of ten, I would turn it around and win. I did not use this technique to intimidate the other person; my intent was to intimidate my fear.

This technique to overcome fear can be applied to numerous activities and situations. Someone with a fear of getting up in front of people could join Toastmasters and practice giving speeches. Someone with a fear of performing could join a theater troupe or take up piano lessons and participate in recitals. Someone with a fear of heights could learn to climb or rappel. The empowering experience of overcoming your fears will extend beyond that specific area in which it was learned. The memory of that triumph is stored in the physical, mental, and emotional body and can be accessed when needed, much like a reference library.

Envision a woman, Laura, who overcame her fear of heights by attending an Outward Bound program in the Rockies. When she returns to work after her trip, she is betrayed by another woman who takes credit for her work and steals her ideas. Laura, a Scholar-King-Server, doesn't like conflict and would rather fume at home than confront the other woman. This time, Laura may not be able to avoid confrontation. She may be passed over for a promotion because of the other woman's actions. Laura's anger rises, and she remembers that not too long ago she climbed a one hundred-foot cliff. She was deathly afraid and fell several times before she had the courage to advance even twenty feet on the wall.

She remembers her instructor telling her she could do it, but she didn't have to, and that he would catch her if she fell. The instructor told Laura to look up, not down, and to be proud of how high she had climbed. Laura got back on that wall and inched her way up to the top. At the crux, a rounded lichen-covered bump, she fell. Fear gripped her again; she was seventy-five feet off the ground. Then instead of looking down, she looked up into the faces of the rest of her group. They shouted words of encouragement: "Laura, you are one bad-ass climbing mama!" And she thought, "Yes, I am!" From that point, she muscled her way to the top. It wasn't pretty, but she made it. She made it by seeing the possibilities. Even with shaky legs and arms and a ferociously beating heart, she saw herself as a climber rather than someone who couldn't.

She didn't know how she was going to do it, but she knew she needed to see herself as someone who could confidently ask for what she wanted. She wanted credit for her own work. Laura also knew she had to confront the woman at work or the woman would never stop sabotaging her.

She started with what she knew and focused on the positive experience of climbing from the Outward Bound trip. She said to herself, "Laura, you are one bad-ass mama! No one is going to steal your ideas. You are in charge of your destiny." She then talked to her boss and confronted the woman with her behavior. Eventually, the woman transferred to another department, and Laura landed her boss's job. Now, on her days off, Laura can be found climbing at the local crag.

Laura demonstrated the courage to face her fears and to confront. It took the Outward Bound experience for her to gain enough self-confidence to be able to go back to work and say what she needed to say to the woman who was abusing her at work. When she finally stood up for herself, however, the other woman felt uncomfortable, backed down, and eventually left. Laura felt empowered and was able to realize her vision for herself when she put her energy towards making things better for herself instead of allowing someone else to use her.

Courage to Confront

When you confront or give feedback to someone else, it is really telling them 100 percent about you and only 50 percent about them. We tend to focus on what interests us. For example, if I tell you that it irritates me that you're always late and you talk too much, I am telling you that I value timeliness and quiet. I might also be telling you that because you talk so much I can't get a word in myself and that I need some space to be heard. Another thing that I could be telling you is that I like predictability and structure (being on time). I value efficiency, and excessive talking seems to be a waste of time to me.

The details are not as important as the "intent." Pay close attention when you are giving or receiving feedback to your voice inflections, body language, even the words you choose. Statements carry vastly different meanings depending on the tone and intent with which they are delivered. Even harsh negative feedback can be softened by the tone of your voice. Before giving feedback or confronting someone, rehearse the information with another person and ask your listener to honestly assess how you come across. If it isn't what you intend, practice conveying the information in a different way.

"A fundamental law of confrontation states, 'When you avoid confronting something today, you create a bigger problem tomorrow.' Whenever we back away from confronting a difficult issue, it doesn't disappear or get better on its own," says Robert Staub. "It festers, grows, and undermines our power. When we avoid confronting painful situations or problems in relationships, we inflict damage on our souls and compromise our integrity.

"We may deal with a small issue today and feel a small amount of pain, or we may deal with a greater issue and face greater pain later. When we avoid confronting a problem, it doesn't disappear or go away. Instead, its impact on us grows, the potential pain grows, a pattern unfolds, and when the inevitable moment of reckoning comes, the pain is ten times worse as a result of our avoidance."[22]

Acting Courageously

A lesson in courage came to me quite profoundly when I was twenty-seven. I had become a successful competitive runner and was quite addicted to my routine of running fifty miles a week, plus weight training, aerobics classes, and bike riding. Gradually, my right knee gave way, and I was told I might not ever be able to run again. I was devastated. I begged the surgeon to operate, to do something, anything, so that I could resume my running. He told me the only thing he could do was put me in an immoblizer cast; in time, my knee would heal on its own. I had a severe form of "chrondomalacia" (runner's knee) and it had gone beyond treatment; only rest, complete rest, would help. The surgeon suggested I take up swimming. In fact, he said it was the only exercise I was permitted to do.

Swimming! The very thought of swimming laps struck terror in me. I felt claustrophobic and panicked. Not being able to swim was one of my deep dark secrets. I made excuses to avoid swimming laps with friends in college. It was a lifelong cover-up.

It began when I was two years old and was found drowning at the bottom of a community pool. My mother had left me in the care of a sixteen year old who was more interested in boys than in watching a toddling two-year-old girl. The lifeguard rescued me and gave me mouth-to-mouth while my panicked mother looked on. I lived, but so did the memory both for me and for my mother. Every time I would get near the water, my mother would shout or cry out. "Don't!" or "Be careful, you can't swim!" and I couldn't.

My mother took me to a woman who had a good reputation for

teaching swimming and who promptly threw me into the deep end of the pool. I panicked and thought I was drowning all over again. I was so frightened that I fought and cried and told my mother I would never go back to see that woman again. Eventually, I learned to dog paddle and could fake my way across one length of the pool.

My embarrassment about swimming stayed with me until my doctor forbid me from running and I was forced to face the local YMCA pool. I tried to swim at the Y three times a week, but was making little progress. Each time I got in the pool, my heart would beat wildly. My legs would sink, and I felt like a lead weight. I felt as if I couldn't get to the other side fast enough and that I might drown.

Then one day I noticed an older man, probably in his eighties, walking slowly to the pool. He struggled from the locker room to the pool using a walker. Slowly, step by step, he placed his walker a little in front of his body, moved his feet forward, then balanced himself and repeated the process painstakingly until he reached the pool.

When he entered the water, it was also a slow process, as was his swimming. He swam, or more like dog-paddled, slowly from one end of the pool to the other without stopping. He never looked at anyone else, never spoke to anyone. His body would sometimes sink so low that it seemed as if he were walking across the pool instead of swimming, but still he kept on.

I became fascinated with this man. I wondered what drove him to go through such a laborious task every day when swimming seemed to be so difficult for him. Day in and day out, he performed the same agonizingly slow ritual—walking to the pool, lowering himself into the water, and then swimming across the pool. It brought tears to my eyes watching him take five minutes to swim one length that would take an average swimmer less than thirty seconds.

Over the weeks, I experienced a range of emotions toward him. At first, I was curious, then I progressed through pity to anger (that he could have a lane exclusively to himself each day) to respect. He became a constant in my pool life. I could count on him like clockwork. Always the same routine. Always the same lane. The same amount of time. I began to see him as my hero. If he could do it, so could I.

I added one lap, then two. I eventually swam a half mile. Then I began to swim faster. I learned to breathe on both sides. I learned to do breaststroke, the butterfly kick, and a flip turn. All this I learned, while the old man at the other end of the pool continued his methodical water routine every day.

He swam on one side of the pool. I swam on the other. He never acknowledged my presence. I never spoke to him. He never got any faster as I was progressing to become a better swimmer. I began to feel stronger, more confident, not only in swimming but in other parts of my life as well. I didn't seem to feel so depressed about my running, and I began to feel that I had options.

Each day before I began my swim, I would look over to make sure he was there. Sometimes I would look over to see if he was watching me, if he knew about my progress. I wondered if he thought about me, because I surely thought about him. I wondered if he noticed how far I had come.

Then one day he didn't show up for his daily swim. Concerned and alarmed, I asked the lifeguard where he was. The lifeguard shrugged and said, "Who?" No one else seemed to know or even seemed to miss him. Lifeguards changed, and the new faces didn't seem to appreciate the days and weeks of swimming this man had been going through. These faces didn't know how profoundly this man had impacted my life; impacted my life without a word, without a sound, without any acknowledgment of my presence.

Later, I found out that he had a stroke and was unable to swim. By then, I was training for a triathlon and swimming with the Master swimmers. I had found a new group and left my afternoon swims behind. I regretted that I didn't get to thank him. One afternoon, I went back to the pool and discovered he had returned to swimming. I said, "Excuse me, sir." He looked at me with a vacant look in his eyes. "I don't know if you remember seeing me here at the pool every afternoon during the winter." No answer. He waited patiently. "I just wanted to say thank you for inspiring me to swim. Watching you every day gave me courage. I wasn't a very good swimmer and you encouraged me to keep at it, and now I'm swimming quite well. In fact, I am training for a triathlon!" Still no answer.

At this point, I wondered if he heard me or if the stroke had affected his memory. I began to feel uncomfortable, as if I had made some kind of a mistake. I also felt vulnerable. I had opened up to a total stranger who didn't reciprocate anything I had just communicated. Then I wondered if I had made too much out of the whole thing.

After a long moment, the old man took his hand off his walker and placed it on mine. He looked into my eyes and said, "You're quite welcome." And then turned to make his way to his side of the pool.

From this experience, I was able to face one of my biggest fears and come out on top. I choose this to illustrate the courage to act. The courage to overcome my fear of swimming was inwardly directed, a purely internal dialogue. I struggled with past and present fear, and through the current inspiration of a fellow human, I was able to break through my comfort zone (of not swimming) into a new area of discomfort (swimming) and eventually feel comfortable enough to be able to do a triathlon.

The courage to act means moving towards a challenge, not away from it. It means staring fear in the face and going bravely into the unknown, all the while knowing that you will be a better person when you come out on the other side. It is a power that we all have, but not everyone uses.

> "It takes a lot of courage to be the same person on the outside that you are on the inside."
>
> BARBARA DEANGELIS
> *Author of* How To Make Love All The Time; Secrets About Men Every Woman Should Know; *and* Ask Barbara: The 100 Most-Asked Questions about Love, Sex and Relationships.

Benefiting from Courage

Laura Evans bravely and courageously acted not only to regain her health after being diagnosed with breast cancer in 1979, but also to help other women. After her diagnosis and almost barbaric chemotherapy treatment, she was determined to improve treatment of breast cancer for all women. She lobbied for more humane and nurturing treatment (instead of being quarantined in a sealed bubble for months) and lobbied for funds for breast cancer research which were practically nonexistent at the time.

She combined her love for climbing and mountaineering with her drive to support treatment of breast cancer and founded Expedition Inspiration, an organization dedicated to raising funds for breast cancer research and to supporting and empowering breast cancer survivors. Each year, several mountaineering trips are planned on high mountains all over the world. Breast cancer survivors climb free; proceeds from those who pay go to research. Laura lost her fight in October 2000, not to breast cancer but to a brain tumor, but the vision created from her willingness to act courageously lives on.

> "As a mountaineer, I'm often asked, 'When were you most afraid?' For me, I wasn't hanging off the side of a mountain. Instead, I was in a [hospital] hallway, walking slowly toward what I knew would be my death or my salvation and knowing that what I was about to undergo would be horrible."
>
> LAURA EVANS
> *The Climb of My Life*
>
> *Laura Evans was a breast cancer survivor and the founder of Expedition Inspiration. In January 1995, she co-led a team of forty-three people, including seventeen breast cancer survivors, ranging in age from twenty-two to sixty-two, to summit Aconcagua in the Argentine Andes. At more than 23,000 feet, this is the highest mountain in the Western Hemisphere. In her book,* The Climb of My Life, *Evans chronicles this expedition as well as her own treacherous experience with cancer.*

EXERCISE

Acting Courageously

1. Make the resolution to get past whatever is frightening you, holding you back, or standing in your way.

   What I fear most is: _____

   _____

   _____

   _____

2. Use any technique mentioned to help you overcome your fear. There isn't one perfect way, but if you listen to your intuition, it will guide you to the "best" method for addressing this specific problem.

   My intuition tells me the best way to address this problem is: _____

   _____

   _____

   _____

3. Imagine yourself addressing the issue. What would it look like? How do you feel? Who and what is involved? How long will it take to overcome this problem or fear? Keep a journal and write down your thoughts about the issue. Periodically, review your journal entries to affirm where you see progress and to restate negative thoughts and comments in a positive way. (Instead of saying "I could just shoot myself for taking over that conversation the other day," restate it as "Yes, I did take over the conversation, but at least I'm aware of it. Next time, I can stop myself sooner.")

   Restate your negative thoughts or comments in a positive way: _____

   _____

   _____

   _____

4. Figure out what it will take to energize you to act to come to a resolution with the problem situation. (For example, I was energized to overcome my fear of swimming because it was the only form of exercise that I could do.)

_____

_____

_____

5. Choose your thoughts, words, and decisions carefully. What you think can shape your physical body and your future. Remember also that you only have so much energy. Choose carefully how you want to use that energy. Make a list of the areas you wish to act upon according to your vision for your life.

My vision is: _____

_____

_____

_____

I can realize that vision by acting on the following fears:

1. _____

_____

_____

2. _____

_____

_____

3. _____

_____

_____

Chapter Summary

Having courage means:

➤ Finding and going for your goal.

➤ Persevering to achieve your life task.

➤ Facing the challenge.

➤ Seeing things clearly.

 • Courage to see current reality

➤ Listening to feedback.

 • Courage to be confronted

➤ Learning and growing.

➤ Overcoming fear.

 • Breathe

 • Perform mental rehearsals

 • Meditate

 • Write/journal

 • Face the fear

➤ Giving respectful feedback.

 • Courage to confront

➤ Acting courageously.

If

If you can keep your head when all about you
Are losing theirs and blaming it on you;
If you can trust yourself when all [wo]men doubt you,
But make allowance for their doubting too:
If you can wait and not be tired by waiting,
Or, being lied about, don't deal in lies,
Or being hated, don't give way to hating,
And yet don't look too good, nor talk too wise;

If you can dream—and not make dreams your master;
If you can think—and not make thoughts your aim,
If you can meet Triumph and Disaster
And treat those two impostors just the same:
If you can bear to hear the truth you've spoken
Twisted by knaves to make a trap for fools,
Or watch the things you gave your life to, broken,
And stoop and build 'em up with worn-out tools:

If you can make one heap of all your winnings
And risk it on one turn of pitch—and toss,
And lose, and start again at your beginnings,
And never breathe a word about your loss:
If you can force your heart and nerve and sinew
To serve your turn long after they are gone,
And so hold on when there is nothing in you
Except the Will which says to them: "Hold on!"

If you can talk with crowds and keep your virtue,
Or walk with Kings—nor lose the common touch,
If neither foes nor loving friends can hurt you,
If all men count with you, but none too much:
If you can fill the unforgiving minute
With sixty seconds' worth of distance run,
Yours is the Earth and everything that's in it,
And—which is more—you'll be a [Wo]man, my
    [daughter]son.

RUDYARD KIPLING
1865-1936

Self-Talk

As I stared at the sky, I reflected.
That most of my life
I felt I had to please others.

Would someone like me
Or accept me, if i just was?
I was afraid not.

Sadness the size of a golf ball
Began in my stomach and
Rose up to choke me
Becoming bigger with the
Realization that,

I was compelled to be what I thought
Others wanted me to be.

Now I realize it was exhausting and
Pointless and
Sad.

Would someone love me for just being me?

The answer echoed through my brain:

Perhaps you
  Do not like yourself.
Perhaps you think
  You must do something to be likeable.
Perhaps you are afraid to be
  And let go of the doing.

Sometimes our internal dialogues
Are reflected in our relationships
With other people.

DEBRA J. GAWRYCH
March 2000

CHAPTER FOUR

CHOICES
(HOW NOT TO BE A VICTIM)

ONE OF THE MOST FRUSTRATING THINGS WE FACE as human beings is our lack of perfection. The things we do that drive ourselves—and each other—crazy only serve to keep us from the intimacy and emotional connections we crave. Some of us fantasize about how easy life would be "if only." Others try to control and demand that people around us behave according to the code of our choosing. The tensions brought about by our weaknesses are stumbling blocks, but they also are opportunities to learn and grow. The key word is opportunity; the choice is ours.

The poem at the beginning of this book, "The Truth of the Sisterhood," talks about the frustration that comes when the currents of life continually pull us towards people and lessons we don't like. As we yearn for a more comfortable experience, we can get stuck, become frustrated, and begin to feel like victims. Frustration and isolation, the poem says, go away when "we begin to see the possibilities." They disappear when we realize that we have a choice. We can choose to remain in our stuck, powerless place, or we can choose another path, another feeling, another point of view.

Manifesting What We Choose to Create

The creation that comes from choice is called manifestation and simply means that we can create whatever reality we choose. It is up to us to decide how and where we are going to spend our time. Do we choose to whine and moan that we don't have the life or job we want? Or do we go out and do something about it? Do we choose to obsess about a person in our lives who doesn't treat us the way we want to be treated? Or do we stand up and demand to be treated with respect? Do we allow abuse to continue? Or do we speak out and say, "Enough! There is a better way."

Choice is about taking a breath and realizing the possibilities in a situation instead of feeling hopeless. No matter how bleak, how grim, how devastating a situation may be, we always have choice. The most amazing thing about choice is that when we start seeing the situation in a new way and start visualizing a better way for ourselves, the energy shifts and the situation changes. The clearer we are about intent and what we choose, the more the outcome of the change will be what we want. Another caveat to the idea of manifestation is the adage, "Be careful what you ask for, because you might very well get it." Manifestation is a powerful tool; think carefully about the ramifications of what you wish for before you put energy into manifesting it.

For example, a friend of mine is a busy go-getter kind of woman. Her husband was more laid-back and loved to play golf. She often complained that he was boring because all he wanted to do was play golf and wasn't interested in art, going to plays, or expanding his mind by meeting other people or traveling. I pointed out that instead of complaining, she needed to ask for want she wanted, to visualize the possibilities instead of focusing her attention on what she didn't want. She started to put a lot of energy into seeing her husband as a companion in all the things she liked to do even if he wasn't.

Little by little, her husband began to take interest in the things that she liked to do. He started going to art galleries with her when they traveled, and he began to read. Although he still played golf, he picked up a few other sports and became interested in dancing. Slowly, he developed a passion for traveling and seeing other cultures. He researched adventure trips and treks to foreign countries. He sought out scientific expeditions for them to do together. He encouraged her to join a couples dance group with him. And then they started to argue.

She began to feel crowded and suffocated by all of his interests. She wanted to have some time to do what she wanted. All of his attention and his varied interests didn't give her the time and space to do what she wanted anymore. She got what she asked for, but when she started living it, she didn't want it.

What did she do next? She created again. This time in dialogue with her husband, she told him how she felt and they were able to work out an equitable solution where they both could get their needs met. She was able to create what she wanted, but was careful to be more in touch with her needs.

Communicate Feelings and Needs

A seminar on nonviolent communication in Greensboro, North Carolina, recently presented a segment on dialogue. It emphasized one of the key points of communication: to get someone to listen to you, you must first listen to them. To facilitate better understanding, you also must deal with both feelings and needs. You must listen for the other person's feelings and needs, and in turn, clearly state your own feelings and needs. Studies have found that women tend to be more in touch with their feelings, while men are more in touch with their needs. Leaving either out in communication, gives the receiver only part of the story. It is important to communicate both in order for the other person to clearly understand your point of view.

For example, if I have a need not be interrupted when I talk, I could say, "When you interrupt me while I'm talking, I feel cut off and angry. I feel as if what I have to say isn't important to you. I need for you to give me time to finish my thoughts before responding, in order for me to feel that you are paying attention to what I have to say."

If I only communicate my feelings, the other person could be embarrassed or angry that I accused her or him of interrupting me. The next time we talk she or he may feel inhibited and not talk at all.

If I only communicate my need of having time to finish my thoughts, the other person may not understand my tone or the depth of my emotion, regarding being interrupted, and continue with her or his behavior. By communicating both parts of the message—the feelings and needs—we give the specifics of the behavior we would like and emphasize with our tone how important these feelings are to us. By clearly and respectfully communicating, we are exercising the power of choice.

Stumbling Blocks to Communication

Many women tend to remain stuck and not communicate effectively. They choose to be covert rather than communicating openly. Instead of speaking directly to someone about an issue, they may talk to someone else about it. Talking behind someone's back or gossiping is the opposite of empowerment; it is powerless and, unfortunately, takes us away from the closeness of being supportive of one another. This tendency not to be direct stems from fear and can be brought about when we are stuck in habitual, nonproductive behavior patterns. We create these patterns to protect ourselves, but the protection is only temporary. The distortion that comes from these protection mechanisms makes it difficult for us to understand ourselves, let alone understand someone else. It is what is known as "false personality" or delusion. Underneath, our true essence (or trilogy of aspects) is who we really are.

When we are anxious about where we are going to live, how we fit in, and getting what we need, we feel tension. The tension can be so great that it causes pain, which we seek to eliminate. At first, we stumble onto something that helps take the edge off the pain. Perhaps it is adopting a different attitude, taking an aggressive stance, and beating the pain to the punch. It could also be withdrawal and numbing ourselves to the pain around us. These adaptive patterns don't take away or heal the roots of the pain. Instead, they become unconscious habits that we continue even if they stop serving their purpose. We can become so distorted by these coping patterns that they blind us to knowing our true selves.

Stumbling Blocks Keep Us From Realizing Our True Nature

In the Seven Aspects Model, these patterns are called *stumbling blocks*. Each person has one that is her primary stumbling block. This feature helps you cope, at first, but it also sets up future difficulties or distortions that you eventually must address if you are to fulfill your lifetime goals. In other words, realizing your stumbling blocks is a handy guide to what you need to work on as person to grow. If a woman has the stumbling block of arrogance, she may appear to be "stuck up" to other people. When in reality, she uses the appearance of arrogance to cover her feelings of low self-esteem and she really wants people to build her up. Her habitual pattern of coming across as haughty or arrogant may have initially helped stem the pain from her insecurity, but as people avoid her because of her arrogance, she finds herself alone. She may even become the target of snide comments and gossip, "Just who does she think she is anyway?"

Take note of the seven stumbling blocks in the Seven Aspects Model (figure 4.1). To overcome the negative effects of each stumbling block, one can slide to the opposite stumbling block and use the positive characteristics of that stumbling block to help break the distortion caused by the first. If I want to break out of the pattern of impatience, I would utilize the positive characteristic of martyrdom (its opposite stumbling block), which is selflessness. This means that I stop thinking that everything I do is the center of the universe. If I'm late, the meeting will go on. If I take time to fix something, it is an act of giving rather than pushing my own agenda.

The negative characteristic of impatience as noted in the chart is intolerance. Picture a mother trying to get three children ready for school.

"It's time to get up."

Ten minutes later: "I said it's time to get up, NOW! You're going to be late."

Ten minutes later: "Are you still in bed? What is wrong with you? Get up and get dressed now. Your little brother is ready, and he is only seven! I expect more from a ten-year-old."

109

Ten minutes later. Now yelling, "OK, THAT'S IT! I'M LEAV-
ING IN TEN MINUTES, WITH OR WITHOUT YOU."

Granted it is frustrating to corral three children and get them to cooperate long enough to get anywhere on time, but someone with impatience will be less tolerant under stress and will need to take an extra breath to stay centered. What helps is to allow time to stand still. Create the sense of selflessness, as if self doesn't exist. When the image and ego are taken out of the situation, impatience goes away. Suddenly, the burden is now on the children. What is the worst thing that will happen? The children are late for school? Okay, who loses? They do. The carpool has to wait and gets so tired of waiting they refuse to pick the kids up anymore? Then the children have to ride the bus and won't be able to participate in some of the after-school activities they like to do. Selflessness comes when the mother is no longer embarrassed or feels the need to make her children do something according to her timetable. This does not absolve the kids from needing to follow rules and have consequences, but it takes away the seductiveness of the habitual pattern of coercing and being intolerant of the children because they aren't the way the mother wants them to be.

Note that for every stumbling block, there is a positive and negative expression of it. To balance the negative characteristic of a stumbling block, we must slide to the positive characteristic of its opposite feature. This is the case in every stumbling block except stubbornness, which stands alone. To overcome the negative characteristic of obstinacy of the stumbling block of stubbornness, one would need to slide to the positive characteristic of determination.

FIGURE 4.1

The Seven Aspects Model: Stumbling Blocks[1]

INSPIRATION		ACTION	
+Humility	+Pride	+Selflessness	+Daring
Self-deprecation	**Arrogance**	**Martyrdom**	**Impatience**
-Abasement	-Vanity	-Victimization	-Intolerance
EXPRESSIVE		**ASSIMILATION**	
+Sacrifice	+Appetite	+Determination	
Self-destruction	**Greed**	**Stubbornness**	
-Suicidal	-Voracity	-Obstinacy	

FIGURE 4.2

Percentages Within the Population[2]

Self-deprecation	10%
Self-destruction	10%
Arrogance	15%
Greed	15%
Martyrdom	15%
Impatience	15%
Stubbornness	20%

The stumbling block varies from individual to individual in varying degrees of intensity. For one person, it could be mild, another intense. The effects of the stumbling block can be erased through observing it, seeking to understand your reactions, and choosing another way of dealing with a given situation. In this way, you can break out of old patterns.

A stumbling block can keep you from achieving your goals and can slow down the speed of your growth. Each stumbling block has underlying fears:

Stumbling Blocks and Their Underlying Fears[3]

Self-Deprecation	The fear of being inadequate.
Arrogance	The fear of being judged.
Self-Destruction	The fear that life is not worth having.
Greed	The fear of not having enough.
Martyrdom	The fear of being a victim.
Impatience	The fear of missing out.
Stubbornness	The fear of change.

At times we may go in and out of any of the stumbling blocks, but will tend to have one that is particularly problematic for us. The stumbling blocks tend to work in pairs. A woman who is impatient and intolerant may also slip into feeling like a victim. A woman who is self-destructive and who feels that her life is not worth living may also believe that she doesn't have enough. Those with stubbornness as the primary stumbling block will be resistant to change.

It is possible to deal with your primary stumbling block, and not continue the issues surrounding it. It is also possible to work through the issues of your primary stumbling block and pick up another to work on. The idea is that to some degree each stumbling block serves as a reminder of what we need to work on to learn, grow, and reach whatever goal we set for ourselves for our lifetime.

A Brief Look at the Stumbling Blocks

Self-Deprecation

A woman assumes her self-worth is low. This woman often apologizes for something, even before she does it. "I really don't know what I'm talking about but…" or "Gosh, I'm really stupid." Or "That was really dumb of me." Other people try to build her up, but after a while, they feel frustrated and stop. This perpetuates a self-fulfilling cycle of inadequacy and low self-esteem that can be broken through self-awareness and empowerment exercises.

The positive characteristic of self-deprecation is humility; the negative is abasement or putting oneself down. Mother Teresa's self-effacing remarks upon being awarded the Nobel Peace Prize are a good example of humility or the positive pole of self-deprecation. Other famous people who have shown the positive side of self-deprecation are: Bridget Fonda, Michael J. Fox, Hugh Grant, Teri Garr, Joni Mitchell, and Julia Ormond.[4]

Arrogance

Women who are shy or have low self-esteem sometimes mask these feelings by creating a veneer of seemingly high self-worth or an air of superiority. "Let me tell you how and what I am. I am important and surely you can see that and treat me accordingly."

Women with this stumbling block will need to have a great deal of attention centered on them. They live with the fear that others will pass judgment on them and find them lacking in some way. In their minds, the best defense is an offense. They have already passed judgment on themselves, so they freely pass judgment on others before it can be passed on them. Both arrogance and self-deprecation are sourced in low self-esteem; this is a valuable place from which to learn lessons about self-acceptance and self-worth. Famous people who have displayed arrogance are: Joan of Arc, Gertrude Stein, Ernest Hemingway, Muhammad Ali ("I am the greatest"), Melanie Griffith, Madonna, Val Kilmer, Jodie Foster, Ralph Fiennes, Cleopatra, and Cindy Crawford.[5]

Self-Destruction

This stumbling block is the act or motivation to harm oneself either physically or emotionally. Self-destructive individuals believe that life is not worth living. This is seen most evident in alcoholics, drug abusers, and wild daredevils. This stumbling block goes hand in hand with the fear of losing control. Women who are self-destructive may take high risks to prove they can control an extreme situation, for example, a woman who flirts with prescription drugs beyond the intended use, a mountaineer who repeatedly exposes herself to life-threatening situations as on Mount Everest, or a compulsive gambler. The self-destructive tendencies can be checked by sliding into this stumbling block's positive characteristic, sacrifice, or the positive characteristic of the opposite stumbling block, greed (appetite).

In the extreme, self-destructive individuals take greater and greater risks until they eventually die. Well-known public figures with self-destruction as their stumbling block include Marilyn Monroe, Judy Garland, Vincent van Gogh, Jimi Hendrix, EmmyLou Harris, Janis Joplin, Jim Morrison, Jean-Paul Sartre, Andy Warhol, and Drew Barrymore.[6]

Greed

Greed is the experience of wanting or desiring and fearing that there will not be enough to go around. This is a poverty consciousness that no matter how much one has, more is desired. Greed can be manifested either physically in the desire for food, sex, money, alcohol, etc. or emotionally, as in the desire for more and more experiences. Women in greed can put off other people by their relentless pursuit of satisfaction. They can be driven and possessed by their cravings.

Greed can be eliminated by confronting the fear of lack and naming the obsession for what it is. The Expressive Aspects of the Artisan and Storyteller are often drawn into the stumbling block of greed.

In the positive pole, greed is an appetite and allows abundance. It allows one to experience having things in great quantity and not feeling guilty about it. In the negative pole, greed is a voracious bottomless pit.

Famous people with greed as a stumbling block are: Bette Midler, Sandra Bullock, Timothy Leary, Nicole Kidman, Ricki Lake, Jacqueline Kennedy Onassis, Don Johnson, Whoopi Goldberg, Kirsten Dunst, Michael Douglas, Hillary Clinton, and Kim Alexis.[7]

Martyrdom

A woman with this stumbling block will put herself through needless suffering. She will feel as if she is a victim of a situation and that it is beyond her control. Martyrdom stems from the fear that she is not free, but is trapped by circumstances or by another person.

One can be a noisy or quiet martyr. The noisy ones complain loudly about their lot in life. The quiet ones suffer silently and act as if their suffering is too great to describe. Martyrs act like victims. This can have the effect of enraging others to the point of retaliation and actually create a victim situation where one would not otherwise have occurred.

Most of us feel like the martyr at some point in time. If our children yell at us or our car breaks down and we don't have enough money to pay the bills, we may feel like a victim. But people with martyrdom as their stumbling block deal with it on a consistent basis. It takes a great deal of concentration and focus to overcome the victim mentality. In the positive pole, martyrdom acts selflessly. This means giving to others instead of thinking of oneself. The early Christians who gained a place in history by their persecution at the hands of the Romans or the selfless service of St. Francis of Assisi are examples of the positive characteristics of martyrdom. Conversely, martyrdom can be taken to the negative and look like victimization. This happens when someone falls into the "poor me" syndrome and gives her power away. She lives her life with humiliation, real or imagined.

Famous people with martyrdom as their stumbling block are: St. Francis of Assisi, Albert Schweitzer, Yoko Ono, Florence Nightingale, John F. Kennedy, Coretta Scott King, Abraham Lincoln, Joan Baez, and Lynn Andrews.[8]

Impatience

This stumbling block is the feeling of frustration or tension that comes from the fear of missing out. Although a popular trait in our society, it is still a negative. It is difficult to be present in the moment when you are busy rushing towards the next deadline. Someone with impatience is always planning and organizing. It is difficult for her to sit back and enjoy life.

Impatience can lead to problematic situations. Someone who is stuck in traffic can become so impatient that she tries to force her way through traffic to find a way to keep moving and causes an accident. Someone in such a hurry to get a job completed could choose not to check her work and the errors caused by not checking take more time to fix than if the work had been checked thoroughly the first time.

The positive characteristics of impatience suggest a bold, daring way of handling a given situation. For example, instead of meekly waiting in line at customs, the "daring" person would exchange words with the customs agent and be on her way. Conversely, the negative pole of impatience is intolerance. A woman operating from this part of the dichotomy would reject people or situations that are unsatisfactory from her point of view. She would think or say, "How could anyone be so lazy and sit there and watch TV when there is so much to do?" Intolerance is the result of heavy frustration and is the inability to achieve things within the time frame she would like.

Famous people with impatience as their stumbling block are: Kathy Bates, Lucille Ball, Marcia Clark, Betty Ford, Tipper Gore, Dustin Hoffman, Goldie Hawn, Whitney Houston, Diane Keaton, Shirley MacLaine, John McEnroe, and Demi Moore.[9]

Stubbornness

This stumbling block is caused by fear of change, not wanting to let go of one's position. Women with this feature believe they have to take a stand in the face of real or imagined opposition.

The remedy for this stumbling block is the practice of letting go in the face of resistance. Much like the ancient Chinese teaching of Lao-Tze, people with stubbornness are encouraged to become like the water that can erode rock. Look at the water flowing in a creek. The water is flexible. It flows in and around the immutable rocks. The rocks don't change; they are resistant. Instead the water changes shape and is able to continue its flow. Living life to its fullest is about being in the flow. The more energy is allowed to flow, the more energy is created to use in manifesting what you need.

In the positive, stubbornness looks like determination. In the negative, stubbornness looks like obstinacy.

Famous people with the stumbling block of stubbornness are: Barbara Boxer, Glenn Close, Robert Duvall, Chris Evert, Dianne Feinstein, Jane Fonda, Mahatma Gandhi, Don Henley, Janet Reno, and Margaret Thatcher.[10]

After reading each section, determine which one of the stumbling blocks seems to be your primary stumbling block. If you are having trouble determining which one applies to you, think about how you react under stress (see chapter 5, "How We React to

Stress"). Add the information about your primary stumbling block to what you already know about your aspects. These become your foundation for evaluation.

Primary Aspect _____

Secondary Aspect _____

Tertiary Aspect _____

Primary Stumbling Block _____

Use the information you already have about your triad of the Seven Aspects and this new information about your stumbling block as you read the stories and information for the rest of the chapter. Consider how you would have reacted in a similar situation.

Ways to Replace Negative Thinking

Consider the old adage: "Is the glass half-full or half-empty?" Much of what happens to us in life can be viewed through the shades of perspective. How do we perceive what is going on? Will we learn from it? Or will we complain that we are victims and can't do anything about the events in our lives? Earlier in this book, we learned to identify our aspects or personality in terms of how we relate to others. Next, we considered how to apply this information to resolve conflicts. Now we will explore the internal dialogue that sabotages our efforts and find ways to replace negative thinking.

Why do women so often need affirmation from other people to feel that they are okay? One could say that it comes from a lack of self-confidence, but that doesn't seem to be the whole story. Logically, if one feels confident in oneself, then the opinions of others shouldn't carry such weight. However, I believe many women are like me—I feel confident, yet it seems my confidence fades when negative energy is directed my way. I'm vulnerable and emotionally pulled whether the negative energy is obvious (such as taunting comments) or more covertly expressed.

Dealing With a Confidence Buster

Sometimes people will deal a blow to your confidence and they don't even realize what they are doing—it is simply their way. So the question then becomes: Do you try to change the confidence buster or do you change yourself? Do you bring the issue out in the open (and realize the confidence buster may not even be aware there is an "issue" to deal with) or turn this into a lesson for personal growth?

Here's my own experience with a confidence buster. We'll call her Annette. Annette is a Warrior-Artisan-Storyteller with the stumbling block of arrogance. Annette and I were involved in several of the same activities, so we saw quite a bit of each other. Although she never said anything directly to me, she seemed to be uncomfortable in my presence and was usually in a hurry to get away from me. I was puzzled and asked myself what I had done to warrant her behavior. Had I inadvertently said something to offend her?

Her behavior towards me was inconsistent. Sometimes she would appear friendly, and other times it was as if she couldn't stand me. Curiously, my first thoughts were "What did I do wrong?" instead of "What is her problem?" I asked other people if they had similar experiences with her; some people did and others did not. I shrugged and tried to put it out of my mind, but it kept coming up as our paths often crossed.

Finally, I came to the conclusion that standoffish Annette was the one with the problem and that I hadn't done anything to merit her insolent attitude. This worked for awhile, then I would come in contact with Annette and the "What have I done to deserve that?" questioning would start all over again. I can't tell you how many times I went through the cycle of being angry, accepting the behavior, being indifferent, and then getting sucked back into being angry or hurt again.

My husband, who was a patient listener the first few go-rounds, finally said pointedly to me, "Why do you even care? She obviously has a problem. Whether she has a problem with you or she's just an unhappy person doesn't matter. Why do you care what she thinks? She isn't part of your life; she's just an acquaintance. Is she the kind of person you want to be friends with? Is she someone whose opinion you value?" The answer was no. "Then why do you care so much about how she acts towards you? So what if she doesn't like you."

"So what if she doesn't like me!" That rang in my ears. I wasn't a fool.

I knew some people didn't like me. But this time it felt unjustifiable; I hadn't done anything wrong. I didn't deserve the way she treated me.

I spent time alone thinking about the Seven Aspects and determined that we were both Warriors. In our own way, we were silently "warring" with each other. I had a sense that she was jealous of or intimidated by me, but I wasn't sure why. And after a while, I realized I couldn't do anything to change her mind. At that point of total frustration, the only tool left to gain closure over the situation was to deal only with myself.

I sought to understand myself and the situation first by taking a deeper look at our dynamics. I knew my personality type from the Seven Aspects Model and intuitively filled in the blanks for hers.

	Debbie	Annette
Primary Aspect	Warrior	Warrior
Secondary Aspect	Scholar	Artisan
Tertiary Aspect	Priest	Storyteller
Primary Stumbling Block	Impatience	Arrogance

I knew from the above that I tended to be impatient when there was a problem, especially one dealing with emotional issues. I also knew the best way for me to get out of the impatience was to put my "self" or ego aside and look at what I could give unemotionally. My self-limiting beliefs stem from my ego. I also felt some justification because I intuited that Annette was stumbling with arrogance. I knew that it most likely stemmed from low self-esteem, but short of giving me intellectual understanding it didn't help me get past the emotions any better.

Taking a closer look at our dynamics, we differed with respect that my focus was for analytical research and looking for the deeper meaning. With an Artisan Secondary Aspect and Storyteller Tertiary Aspect, Annette was more likely to be a dreamer about possibilities, perhaps even live in a fantasy world and communicate her dreams through stories. The more I thought about our differences, the more I realized that was true. I was deep, and to the point. She told long stories that seemed to drone on and on to build herself up. I was focused more on the facts and shared if I thought it would have some impact on a person or situation.

When I looked closer at my own behavior, I could see a tendency to be judgmental and intolerant when someone wasn't quick enough to get a concept I wished to convey. The more I thought about that, the more I realized that it was exactly the opposite of what I believed in. I was actually being judgmental about other people, especially women who didn't act like me. I realized I was being judgmental about Annette.

My preference would have been to handle the situation out in the open, to tell Annette how I felt and hope that would give her an opportunity to air her feelings, but I didn't believe she would be open to talking with me. I came to the conclusion that I could make a choice. I could choose not to let it bother me, and I could choose to get past it. I didn't feel comfortable in limbo; I needed a resolution.

My relief came in the form of a letter. At the suggestion of a friend, I wrote a letter to Annette, telling her in direct, unedited words how I felt about the way she treated me and what I wanted from her. The letter wasn't sugarcoated. I let her have it with both barrels. I vented and emptied myself of all of the pent-up emotions. After I wrote down my angst, I put the letter away in a memory box and promptly forgot about it. The miracle of writing the letter was that the emotional "hook" was gone. I didn't feel dread at meeting Annette anymore. I didn't care one way or another how she reacted to me. I really believed what my family and friends had been telling me all along. It was her problem, not mine. I felt empowered.

As time went on, Annette's behavior towards me changed. She instigated conversations with me when we ran into each other. Although she still seemed to want to limit the time she talked to me, at least she was making an effort. She seemed to be extending the "tip of the olive branch." I gently encouraged her changes by being friendly, but seldom intruded on her space unless absolutely necessary. We may never be the best of friends, but at least much of the tension that permeated the air when we were together is gone. I enjoy being around Annette now, and she appears to be at ease with me. I learned a lot from working through this situation.

In reality, Annette was a teacher for me. I learned that:

1. I had to value my own feelings.

2. I needed to seek to understand myself and the other person.

3. Sometimes there isn't anything you can do outwardly to change a tense situation.

4. I could only change or control my own thoughts and actions.

5. I had a CHOICE.

As a Warrior, I had the courage to confront her, but that would not have been the best choice of action. It could have given her an external reason to dislike me and given form to feelings that she was having difficulty openly acknowledging. Instead, I worked through the situation on my own, internally, and in the process changed the dynamics of our situation.

Warriors have the instinct to fight unfairness and adversity. I wanted so badly to march right up to Annette and ask her if she had a problem with me. But no, for me that would have been too easy. I had something else to learn.

In this type of situation, a Scholar would be more apt to mediate or work it out through talking. A Storyteller wouldn't have even been bothered, nor would a King. They would say, "It's her problem, not mine." A Server would have been devastated and overwhelmed in the presence of such strong negative feelings directed towards her and retreated, perhaps talking behind her back.

Each aspect brings her own unique means of dealing with negative energy, but every person makes choices. We can choose not to be victims. We can choose to be empowered and to "deal" with tough situations without losing our self-respect.

Thoughts Are Real

As I think back on what happened, I see distinct patterns emerge. When I feel dissonance with someone or something, I direct my energy towards achieving harmony. I consciously or unconsciously seek to resolve the dissonance. Therefore, I am spending a great deal of time and energy on resolving negative energy directed my way, instead of directing my own energy towards positive people and things. It is much like the child who gets attention by misbehaving while the well-behaved child is ignored.

I see this played out over and over again. If I walk into a group situation and sense that another woman in the group has a problem with me, I will first seek to find out the nature of the problem. I may engage that person in a conversation in order for her to get to know me a little better; I hope an inviting attitude will dissipate some of the tension directed towards me.

What is important in this process is the identification of the tension, the clarification of values (or uncovering the real person), and then the release of that tension. To do this is a powerful gift—both for yourself and for the other person. They may never realize what you have done, but in the long run it helps everyone, because there isn't negative energy hanging around anymore.

One of the biggest deceits of society is the belief that if it isn't spoken or written, it isn't real. If someone feels mad or sad, jealous or judgmental, as long as it isn't expressed: it doesn't count. It only takes a quick look at health statistics to refute that thought. How many people in the world suffer from depression, eating disorders, alcoholism, drug addiction, and ulcers? These illnesses often stem at some point from an emotional, mental, personal energy type of disorder. They are either caused or exacerbated by internal negative thought patterns.

We think that thoughts aren't important, but they are very real. Give them enough time and attention and they solidify into belief systems. Our bodies conform to our thoughts. Someone who lacks self-confidence may hunch her shoulders, not look others in the eye when speaking, and not project her voice. Someone who dislikes you may look through you, instead of at you when you are speaking, because she doesn't want to validate your presence.

It is important that we carefully monitor our thoughts. When negative thoughts enter your mind, clear them. You can simply say, "Cancel that thought," or reframe the thought in a more positive way. For example, a frustrated parent may say aloud or to herself, "I'd really like to kill that kid!" But most of us don't mean it literally, no matter the level of frustration. Still, it isn't healthy to leave thoughts hanging like that. Remember thoughts are real. Acknowledge that it isn't something worth keeping and send it on its way. Cancel the thought.

Thoughts can harden and get stuck: "I'm too fat." "How stupid could I be to do that!" "I have to do everything or nothing will get done." "Nobody understands me." These thoughts can take hold and get stuck in our bodies. We may hold them as tension in our muscles (particularly in the shoulders and diaphragm) or in places such as our stomach, heart, lungs, or abdomen. It is a good idea to release this tension through massage, bodywork, and other relaxation techniques.

Bring On the Positive Thoughts

Positive thoughts are equally powerful. Instead of dwelling on negative thoughts, replace them with positive ones. An effective way of identifying your thoughts and changing them is through journaling. When you're trying to identify your thoughts or feelings keep a notebook, laptop, or cassette recorder handy. Record your thoughts without editing them. You may be shocked at what you have recorded. Don't hold back. Be honest. This is for you. No one else needs to read what you write. In fact, a technique that I use is to write in the front of my journal, "The contents of this journal are private and meant only for my personal use. Read this at your own risk. You are responsible for anything that may happen if you read these pages."

EXERCISE

Analyzing Your Thoughts

One effective method for keeping track of your thoughts is to keep a notebook or journal handy with you throughout the day. Try to make a serious effort to record continuous thoughts that affect you physically or emotionally throughout the day. Here's an example:

THOUGHTS	FEELINGS	PHYSICAL REACTION
Oh my gosh, I'm lost!	Panic. Anxiety.	Shoulders tight. Stomach knots. Gasp for breath.
How do I get back to where I need to go? I'm going to be late for the meeting. They'll kill me.	Panic. Anxiety. Fear. Frustration.	Neck and shoulders tighten. Breathing is rapid and shallow. Frantic head movements. Voice louder and higher.
I found the meeting after all. Only ten minutes late. I can live with that.	Relief. Peace. Contentment. Relaxed. Happy.	Stomach feels warm and relaxed. Shoulders relax. Breath is deeper.

Using a tool like this one is an effective means of identifying and analyzing your thought patterns. To make changes, we have to start with identifying the behavior we want to change and record each time the behavior occurs.

By analyzing your thoughts in this systematic, detailed manner, you will be able to identify thoughts, feelings, and their powerful physical reactions by yourself, without relying on someone else to identify them for you.

If you are diligent about monitoring your thoughts, after a while you will be able to identify intent immediately. It will then be easy for you to change the unwanted thoughts. "I'm not good enough" can be transformed into "I'm the best I can be." "I can't stand that person" can be changed to "I feel uncomfortable when I'm around her, so I have a choice. I can choose not to be around her or look for something positive about her. If I have to be with her, at least I can make the best of it."

This is not to say that you deny your feelings. On the contrary, you must be unscrupulously honest. If you dislike someone or something, it does you no good to deny it. Thoughts are real and exist whether you acknowledge them or not. If you don't acknowledge your true feelings, they can get stuck and stored somewhere in your body, which could lead to stress-related illnesses.

Other Techniques for Accentuating the Positive

Reinforcing Positive Thoughts

Reinforcing positive thoughts is an effective way to achieve your goals. Goal setting, by its very nature, involves stating a desired outcome, then outlining steps that will help you reach your goal. To do this, it is important to keep negative thoughts from sabotaging the process. It is helpful to write yourself reminders. Tape them on mirrors, bookshelves, and in the car.

Using Dreamwork

Another effective technique is *dreamwork*. Before going to sleep, visualize your goal. See yourself achieving this goal and go through the motions that lead up to that success. So, for example, if you want to make a great presentation, see yourself making notes for the presentation, writing it, practicing it, getting dressed, walking in front of the group, and presenting your material. Visualize success. See yourself making all the points you'd like to make and the audience carefully attending to your words. Have fun with it! See yourself getting thunderous applause, even a standing ovation. It's your dream; make it as big as you want. It is possible to "will" yourself to dream certain things, but if this seems difficult for you, start by daydreaming. As you learn to guide your daydreams, your subconscious will learn to respond to your request for specific dreams while you sleep.

If you are already able to direct your dreams, lucid dreaming is the next step. In lucid dreaming, you are conscious that you are dreaming while you are dreaming. It has a tremendous advantage to regular dreaming in that you are able to change the course of your dreams while you are dreaming.

When I am lucid dreaming and don't like the outcome of one of my dreams, I say, "Okay, that wasn't so good. Next time I'd like to try_____ at a crucial decision point and dream it through to a new outcome." This is empowering because it trains your subconscious to see that you do have the power to change your life. Once you believe this, both consciously and subconsciously, you are ready to create and experience great things!

Posting Inspirational Reminders

I often write inspirational sayings on pieces of paper and post them around the house. This helps me feel uplifted and keeps me anchored to the positive thoughts I want to maintain throughout the day. When focusing on a goal, I use the same reminders to keep me on track.

Building Support Networks

Because I'm a social person, I will also share my goal with others in order to enlist their support in reaching my goal. Friends call and remind me of my goals. "Are you working on your book?" "How is the book coming?" "Do you need any help with your seminar design?" and "Are you writing two hours every day or are you letting activities and family needs keep you from writing?"

Support is great for everything from running a marathon to trying to improve your relationship with a mother-in-law or spouse. Some of us do better with a broader base of support; others prefer to do it for themselves. The form of support you find most helpful has a little to do with your aspect and a lot to do with whether you are extroverted or introverted, and the degree to which you want and express the need for inclusion.

Extroverts, by their very nature, think by talking. They depend on other people to be their sounding boards and may change their minds several times during the course of a conversation. They work through problems and come up with new ideas by conversing with other people. It is more difficult for them to work in silence and to work alone. Introverts, on the other hand, think internally and express themselves after they have carefully "mulled it over" in their heads. They are reluctant to communicate their problems or feelings until they feel they have a "good handle" on the situation. Neither way of communicating is better than the other.

A few people are equally divided between the two types of expression, but most feel comfortable one way or the other. Knowledge of your preferred mode of expression is helpful in determining how to get rid of negative thoughts and reinforce positive ones.

An extrovert may journal, but at some point may prefer to talk about the thoughts she recorded. An introvert may share her thoughts, but only privately and only after she has already carefully deliberated over what she has written. The introvert would need to have a certain degree of comfort that she understands what is going on before she would share it.

Sometimes the Hardest Choice: Honoring Your Own Needs

How can thought analysis help with choice? Sometimes playing out your response to situations makes the choice clearer. For example, it is easy for me to become overstressed and hard for me to say "no." I am an easy target for fund-raiser volunteer. When I am asked to do a task for a fund-raiser—a task I should turn down because I don't have time—I should analyze my thoughts, before I make a commitment. The internal dialogue goes something like this:

My thoughts: "Oh my gosh, she isn't going to ask me to do something, is she? I was chairman of that fund-raiser for two years and have helped every year they've had it. How much more do I have to give?"

Fund-raiser organizer: "You did such a good job chairing the fund-raiser for the past several years. We really need your expertise."

My thoughts: "Yes, they probably do need me. And it was exciting working on it, if I forget that my family had frozen dinners for six months."

At this point, I am at a crossroads. I can say: "Thanks, I'll see what I can do."

Fund-raiser organizer: "Great. I'll send you some forms to solicit donations." That's when the realization sets in that I have semi-committed myself to a task I really don't want to do. I feel a growing sense of panic. I know my time is limited. If I spend time doing the fund-raiser, I won't have the time to do what I really want and need to do: finish my book. My thoughts tell me how I really feel: overwhelmed, afraid, and trapped.

Or I can take a different path, and see how it would play out differently. In my thoughts, I hear myself saying, "I'd really like to help you, but I can do this job and no more." Suddenly, I've set limits, boundaries. My commitment seems attainable without a "superhuman effort." Instead of panic, I feel satisfaction and a warm feeling that I am helping and at the same time taking care of myself, honoring my own needs.

Setting Clear Boundaries

Part of the process of honoring your own needs includes being able to set clear boundaries. So many of us want the world and other people to take care of our feelings and emotions so that we can "feel" better. We want others to make it okay for us. We don't want the pain and discomfort of tension. We want it to simply go away. We believe that someone else is the cause of our discomfort, and they have to make it better.

Women who are empathetic and nurturing tend to face a special anguish when dealing with this. There are plenty examples of this in my life and the lives of others. The most glaring example in my life is my oldest son. He is a Warrior-Storyteller-Server with the stumbling block of stubbornness. For most of his life, thirteen years, he has demonstrated a bad temper and impatience when told he can't have his way. He shows a lack of respect for authority and a willful disregard for others' feelings when his temper is in full force. He pushes situations past the point of limits to test boundaries and seems to delight in the effect that has on others.

To all this, I must add that when his temper isn't in the way, he is sensitive and caring about the feelings of others and willing to listen. Although emotionally immature at times, he shows tremendous insight into the psychological and subtle inferences in situations between others. He is extremely intelligent and quick to pick up ideas, yet difficult to teach. In short, he is a challenge to parent.

I have tried every technique and read every parenting book I could find about how to deal with a difficult child. The best I've been able to come up with is that I must set firm boundaries. When he blows up, I must be firm with consequences, yet stay out of the way emotionally. This is a difficult balance.

To illustrate, we worked together to draw up a contract for his behavior. The contract stated that he was to respect his parents, do certain chores around the house (such as keep his room clean), and be neat and organized with schoolwork as well as the equipment he needed for extracurricular activities. Additionally, he was expected to tell the truth. He violated the contract within three days and felt the consequences by having extracurricular activities as well as privileges (TV and video games) taken away.

His behavior improved well enough to be able to attend a big swim meet. The morning of the second day of the meet he started acting up again—not being cooperative, not doing his chores, yelling at me. I promptly told him he was going down the wrong path; if he didn't make better choices, he wouldn't be going to the meet. To my way of thinking, he should have taken that as a warning, a wake-up call, and done everything in his power to fulfill his contract to get what he wanted in the long run. Instead, he remained stuck in his anger and escalated the yelling. He gave me ultimatums, such as "I'm not going to do what you've asked until you promise to take me swimming." His anguish was real, but I've learned the hard way that the only way he would learn to work through his emotions would be if I remained steadfast on the boundaries and he didn't go to the meet.

In trying to come up with effective strategies to parent him, I again look to the Seven Aspects Model to assess the dynamics of the situation. My son and I are both Warriors, and neither of us are afraid to do "battle." The real change comes when one of us chooses to be flexible. When one of us is flexible, or like "water flowing over rocks," the other is given the space to come out of his or her intractable position and look for an alternative way of communicating.

My son's Secondary Aspect of Storyteller provides for lively conversations, such as, "Son, are you telling the truth?" or "It would be much better for you if you didn't lie to me." His Tertiary Aspect of Server is where we connect. He is helpful and is genuinely giving at his heart; it is just difficult to see when he is coming from his aggressive Warrior Aspect or when he is staunchly entrenched in his stumbling block of Stubbornness. The negative side of stubbornness is obstinacy; the positive is determination. As he matures, he will find his communications more effective when he is willing to be determined, but flexible. Hopefully, he will integrate this into his being as he experiences success with his flexibility.

After several years of holding to firm boundaries, he finally seems to be understanding, at age thirteen, that even if he "wins the battle" he may lose in the long run. He is beginning to give up the "need to be right." Perhaps in another few years, he will begin to make the best choices on the front end, but for now, we'll settle for the awareness.

As a parent and a woman, I feel empowered that I have been able to stay centered while setting firm, clear boundaries with my son. It is a satisfying feeling when I am able to do this, and it serves to anchor the knowledge within me that we do have choices.

Laugh a Little

Another point to make about choice is it is helpful to have a sense of humor. Sometimes as women, we take ourselves too seriously. To help with choice, pick up a good book, a comedy. Watch a funny movie. Laugh. See the humor in the situation, no matter how bad it is. A particularly funny book is *The Sweet Potato Queen's Book of Love*. It is a wickedly funny book about women, men, and life. If anything, this tongue-in-cheek guide teaches us how to laugh. It is a great cure for a perpetually angry or depressed outlook on life.

Comic actor Tom Hanks offers good advice for those who like to play the victim role. One night on *The Tonight Show*, he told told Jay Leno that he didn't believe in making New Year's resolutions. Instead he believed in creating a "philosophy" for the coming year. This year his philosophy was "Deal with it!" Hanks demonstrated how all-purpose this phrase could be: "Deal with it" could be used in anger. It could also be used when someone had a problem and didn't want to "deal with it" anymore. It could be used matter-of-factly to shorten a conversation.

So many people play the victim role, they want someone else to make it better for them. Don Henley said it so well in a popular song he wrote to show his disgust for talk shows (such as Jerry Springer), which make a living from people whining and being victims. He sang, "Get over it! Get over it!"

I would go one better and say, "Deal with it!" Make different decisions. Make new choices!

Chapter Summary

Exercise your power of choice by:

➤ Seeking to understand your stumbling blocks.

➤ Monitoring your thoughts.

➤ Journaling.

➤ Reinforcing positive thoughts. Use words, art, or music to keep your thoughts positive and on track to achieve your goals.

➤ Using dreamwork.

➤ Honoring your intuitive feelings.

➤ Having a nurturing support base:

• Friends

• Family

• Groups

• Church, etc.

➤ Setting clear boundaries.

➤ When stuck, realizing you have a choice. Choose something different, something better.

➤ Having a sense of humor.

Dissonance

Words fly
Propelled forcefully as if
Blown from the horn
Of a large brass instrument
Clashing and clanging
A discordant cacophonous sound
Sharp against flat
Tumbled and jumbled
Intermittent sounds
Each grabbing for space
Unwilling—to share a point in time
Not willing—to be in tune
Refusing—to be in harmony.

DEBRA J. GAWRYCH
April 20, 1993

CHAPTER FIVE

CONFLICT RESOLUTION

A S WOMEN, WE OFTEN FIND SITUATIONS OF CONFLICT in our relationships. Something happens in encounters with a co-worker, a sister, a mother-in-law, or a friend. Something is said and we react. Often times we react in a way that not only hurts the other person, but ourselves as well. Instead of resolving conflict, we perpetuate it. We find ourselves *stuck* and are helpless to change. We don't know how to get out of the combative situation.

Understanding comes when we're feeling the most afraid. It comes when the only thing we want is for the situation to go away. When we need a rest, feel depressed and full of despair. At this time, the darkest hour, we need to remind ourselves: "There is a way out!"

If you don't know what else to do, remember this:

> *If you always do what you've always done,*
> *You'll always get*
> *What you've always gotten.*

Change something. Anything.
Your tone. Your words.
Your attitude. Your look.
Smile.

The point is that when you change, even a small amount, the other person *has* to change. This change may be for the better or it may be for the worse, but it *will be different.*

The Seven Aspects come in to play when we try to come to an understanding about ourselves and our relationships with other people. The very person in your life that torments you the most can be your greatest teacher. It is perhaps easiest to understand when we're trying to resolve conflict.

Imagine a typical workplace situation described in terms of the Seven Aspects. A Warrior starts a meeting. She is full of drive and ideas to organize and structure the meeting. Several members of the group bristle. They may be thinking:

"Just who does she think she is?"

"So bossy. So pushy."

"Who is she trying to impress?

"Control. Control. Control. She always has to be in charge!"

When members of the group stray from the main topic and the Warrior tries to bring the meeting back on track, the Warrior may reprimand them, "That's all very well and good, but we're discussing the marketing strategy right now. We can't afford to waste time discussing unrelated topics. I suggest you schedule a meeting for another time if you need to discuss these other topics."

The resulting unspoken reactions from group members could be:

"How crudely put." (Artisan)

"So narrowly focused. What about the big picture?" (Priest)

"This is no way to run a meeting. I could do a much better job. I'd better take control." (King)

"How boring. We need a few jokes to liven up the place."
(Storyteller)

We can see how the personality of the various aspects comes in to play, and how an astute meeting facilitator would use this information to her advantage. The Warrior facilitator in this case would do well to understand the dynamics of the group before jumping in to structure the meeting. (Warriors have a tendency to be impulsive.) It would be more effective for her to lead with cooperation, instead of forcing her ideas on the group. How does she gain cooperation from the group members? By recognizing their strengths and using them.

A Scholar is effective in mediating and being a neutral party during meetings. It is as if her mere presence helps the other aspects get along and communicate more effectively. Therefore, it is wise to include a Scholar when planning a meeting.

A Priest or King would be best to lead the group, especially for her skills in strategic guidance. The Warrior may feel more comfortable structuring around the broader focused leadership of Priests and Kings.

This information can be a useful tool in structuring a meeting for positive outcomes before conflict occurs. Through careful planning and an awareness of personality tendencies, it is possible to change the outcomes of situations that are continually wrought with conflict.

This analysis can be put to use in nonwork situations. A family with a Server mother who is constantly giving her time and energy to one child (Storyteller). The other children—a King, a Priest, and a Warrior—are jealous, but handle their feelings in different ways.

King: "Mom, you're wearing yourself out doing all that work for Storyteller. We all pitch in to help, including Storyteller. I'll call everyone and work out a schedule so it is not so hard on you."

Priest: "Mother, what kind of an example are you setting if you're always running around taking care of Storyteller? It's important for you to say no once in a while. I've got a book on setting boundaries I'd like you to read."

Warrior: "Mom, for heaven sakes, you are letting Story-teller run all over you! Why can't you say no? It's time to set your foot down and let Story-teller feel her own consequences."

Although, each aspect has valid points, their presentation of their concerns tend to be different. For the sake of the example, the comments are exaggerated characterizations of what they would most likely say. Yet each one of the children could go one step further. After each voices her concerns, she could ask for what she wants. One of the first steps in resolving conflict is to be clear about what you are feeling and what you need from the other person or the situation that is causing you stress.

Dealing With Difficult People

What about people who are out to get you or rub you the wrong way? You know the ones. People who exist to let you know how wonderful they are, and how lacking you are. People who have everything money can buy and want you to know it. People who are so self-centered all they talk about is themselves. People who take credit for something you've done. People who gossip and lie. The list goes on and on. Merely being in their presence creates conflict and tension.

The irony is that any one of "us" can be one of "those" annoying people. All of us have been annoying at some point in our lives. We've all rubbed somebody the wrong way. So, at the same time that we're irritated with someone, somebody else could be irritated with us. While we're irritated because our neighbor isn't as friendly as we'd like, our neighbor may be saying they wish we'd leave them alone and give them their privacy. A big part this book is devoted to the concept that living together with other people doesn't work well when we pass moral judgments.

Conflict resolution is looking at both sides of the "annoying people" issue. Both sides have their viewpoint. When judgment is taken out of the equation, neither side is right and neither side is wrong. They are just different. This is the starting point for resolving conflict.

Begin with the ability to view an issue from another, perhaps even opposing viewpoint. When you do this, you can begin to understand how the other person thinks and see why she does the things she does. This understanding helps the light shine through the glass window of the sisterhood. The cloudiness and darkness of tension burn away as the light of understanding shines through it. You can see a new way of acting, a new path—one of resolution and one that comes from an "enlightened" way of thinking.

Forgiveness

Lord, teach us to forgive:
To look deep into the hearts
Of those who wound us,
So that we may glimpse,
in that dark, still water,
not just the reflection
of our own face
but yours as well.

SHEILA CASSIDY
Laughter, Silence and Shouting:
An Anthology of Women's Prayers

How We React to Stress

Stress can cause anyone to react irrationally and far from their best in a given situation. Conflict can cause stressful reactions, and stress can cause conflict. The following is a brief listing of how each aspect is likely to behave during periods of stress.

King
- Demanding, arrogant
- Indignant that her benevolence is not recognized
- May live excessively and become overindulgent to satisfy needs

Warrior
- Coercive, quick-tempered, argumentative, impatient
- Can resort to intimidation to get her way
- Can become too intensely focused on a project and not consider other people or their feelings
- Can be judgmental towards someone who doesn't grasp things as quickly as she does

Artisan
- Withdraws into fantasy world
- Self-indulgent, moody
- Creates her own negative reality by putting herself down
- Can become scattered and not be able to focus on a task long enough to see it through
- Feels physical symptoms of emotions that have not been dealt with properly

Storyteller
- Tries to justify her actions
- Grabs for attention, egocentric
- Forces her opinion on others
- May be deceitful in order to get what she wants

Server
- Overextends herself, then lashes out or pouts because others have not taken care of her
- Allows people to trample her feelings or use them then retaliates in a covert, vengeful way, instead of being straightforward
- Afraid to set clear boundaries and can be passive-aggressive
- Acts like a victim
- Manipulative/controlling behind the scenes

Priest
- Whines
- Overzealous, forces her beliefs on others
- Promotes her own agenda, regardless of the impact on others
- Wants to fix everything, whether or not she is asked to help
- Because she is so idealistic, may become totally opposite under stress—fatalistic, pessimistic, and accusatory
- Flaky, may resort to extreme views or thinking

Scholar
- Withdrawn
- May be argumentative using logic or facts in order to get space to de-stress
- Likes to appear knowledgeable and confident even when she doesn't know what she is talking about or is only gathering data but, under stress, this obsession increases and leaves the impression of arrogance
- May try to control situations with words or knowledge
- May appear out-of-the-mainstream or too theoretical as a means of distancing herself from others

EXERCISE

Understanding the Dynamics of Conflict Using the Seven Aspects

In this exercise, you will learn how to step back from conflict and evaluate what is happening and why. You do this by:

1. Identifying your Primary Aspect and the Primary Aspect of the person with whom you are in conflict.

2. Noting the characteristics of each aspect and how they may be opposing.

3. Considering ways of improving the situation based on your new understanding.

STEP ONE: Take a moment to reflect on a situation in which you have experienced conflict with someone. Read "How We React to Stress" on page 140 to help you judge the Primary Aspect of the other person. Also use your intuition as a guide. Then complete the following as it pertains to this situation:

My Primary Aspect _____
Other Person's Primary Aspect _____
Summary of the Conflict _____

STEP TWO: List the characteristics of each person, who is causing conflict. Again use "How We React to Stress" as a resource.

	You	**Other Person**
Characteristics _____		_____
_____		_____
_____		_____
_____		_____

STEP THREE: After listing the characteristics, look at possibilities for resolving the conflict. Jot down a few notes on things you can do differently to turn this situation around.

_____

Let's look at some examples of how this exercise can work.

STEP ONE: In this conflict situation, there is a Warrior and Priest who are working together on a project. The Priest is the leader who is out-front with her vision, and the Warrior is the committee member who distrusts the Priest's direction and suspects ulterior motives.

STEP TWO: What are the characteristics exhibited by both women in this situation?

Warrior	Priest
Speaks the truth	Bends the truth to accomplish goal
Loyal	May misuse loyalty
Abrupt	Smooth
Direct to a fault	Indirect
Impulsive	Contemplates decisions

STEP THREE: In the above example, the Warrior doesn't trust the Priest. The Warrior could use her natural tendencies to be forthright and truthful to address this issue with the Priest.

Example 1

Warrior: "I'm having a little trouble understanding how doing X will lead us to Y and A. Can you help me?"

Priest: "Glad you brought that up. You see, in order to achieve our overall goal of Y and Z, we need everyone to buy in to the process."

Warrior concludes that the Priest is leading for the good of the group rather than for her own personal gain.

Let's look at another conflict situation. This time a Warrior (the daughter) and Priest (the sister-in-law) are butting heads over a family matter: an anniversary party.

Example 2

Warrior: "What gives with this party you're having for Mom and Dad?"

Priest: "I thought it would be great to get the family together to celebrate not only Mom's birthday, but also their fortieth wedding anniversary and our nephew's tenth birthday, which are all in the same month. It's so hard to get us all together; I thought it would be fun to make it one big party."

Warrior: (who thinks the party is really a way for her sister-in-law to butter up her parents in order to get money to help finance renovations she and the Warrior's brother are doing on their home) "Hmm. Plus it wouldn't hurt to get in Mom's and Dad's good graces, would it?

Priest: "Sure that would be great, but our loan came through. I just realized it was their fortieth wedding anniversary, and they won't be around forever. Why not celebrate while they're still healthy and we can do it as a *whole* family, rather than wait to get together when there's a problem or they're sick."

Warrior considers that she may have been wrong about her sister-in-law's motives.

Use this exercise and these examples to guide you to a better understanding of situations and people that cause you stress due to conflict.

Office Power Plays

Some years ago I was hired as a systems analyst for a major bank in the Southeast. My department was called Funds Management and handled investments for the bank and its customers. At that time, in the mid-1980s, it was the most respected department in the bank. Traders and investment salespeople on the trading floor were treated like gods. My initial position was in the operations area, and we were most definitely *not* treated like gods. Our job was to support and serve.

I was given a large corner office and put under the tutelage of a wise woman manager who had worked her way up from the ground floor.

Unknown to me, Beth the manager had been mentoring another young woman named Sharon who was a section head in the operations area. Sharon was not happy about my arrival on the scene.

At first, I was charmed by the attention I was getting from both Beth and Sharon. Sharon came into my office as often as she could, asking questions about what I was doing, asking me to lunch, and talking to me about the importance of women banding together to network. Then I noticed the long stares, the cold shoulder when Beth wasn't around, and finally, the memos. I was quickly indoctrinated into the politics of memo wars, which meant, "Write a memo to cover your ass and if possible make someone else look bad so you can look good."

Meetings were set, and I wasn't notified. Sharon's sabotage was effective; people began to question my professionalism and my ability to do the job. My job as a systems analyst required that I was a liaison between all persons and departments using our systems. Systems design requires a lot of cooperation, and I wasn't getting it.

It became quickly apparent that Sharon wanted me to look bad. Exacerbated, I went to my manager, who smiled and said, "Well, it's about time you faced the real world. I wondered how long you were going to let this nonsense go on without fighting back."

It shocked me that Beth already knew and was just waiting for me to take the initiative. Old tapes of "it's not fair" played in my mind. I felt like I was above all this. I was the MBA student, the highly paid brainpower brought in to elevate the level of operations in the department. Why did I have to deal with the pettiness of some woman who didn't have anything better to do with her time than write memos and look for a chance to catch me making a mistake? Looking back now, I'm grateful that my manager listened to me complain and moan about what to do, but encouraged me to get tough and figure out how to deal with it in my own way. And I did.

I started by getting to know Sharon better. I looked for the good things about her character and used those to build a construct of who she really was. At the same time, I noted her weaknesses and filed them away for future reference. These I would use as either things to avoid or to counter her attacks if needed.

As I got to know her better, I learned that Sharon had an art history degree (unusual for someone in banking operations). She had one child; in fact, her water broke while she was at work and she still kept working until they forced her to go to the hospital. I learned that trappings of success were important to her. She needed the accoutrements of success such as a large corner office, a title, and the audience of upper management in order to feel like she was important. Blindly, she would do anything within her power to get them. I saw her one-track focus, her need for perfection, her drive, and her coolness towards the people who worked for her. She wasn't liked. The boys on the trading floor thought she was a "witch," and in general, people saw her for what she tried to hide: her insecurity and fear at being exposed.

I believe she would have been shocked to know this. I think Sharon felt that she was a hard worker who deserved more than she was getting. I also believe she felt she was kind to others, but others didn't see it that way.

The more I got to know her, the more she showed her desire for the appearance of power. Every chance I got, I would explain to Sharon that a corner office meant nothing to me, that I wasn't interested in being head of anything in operations, that my plans were elsewhere, that all of this was just a training ground for me. It was my way of trying to diffuse the tension.

To this day, I don't know if it helped immediately, but I can say that things between us did change dramatically. She eventually left the bank a kinder, gentler, less self-absorbed woman and considered me a good friend. Looking back on what transpired in our short two years together, I think we made a big impact on each other's lives. She taught me things I needed to learn in order to deal with people who want power or success at my expense. I taught her that she could trust another woman and that she could get what she wanted on her own merits rather than by tearing others down. I didn't have to read about it in a book. I lived it, and that experience is well worth telling.

What I learned from Sharon helped me develop a "template" for dealing with people who are negative and not going to make interactions easy.

Dealing with People Who Want Power and Success at Your Expense

1. **Know yourself before you act.** Focus your attention inside to determine what you really want before taking any action. This will help you to be proactive rather than reactive. It will also help you to determine which of the techniques you need to employ in any given situation.

2. **Seek to understand the other person and the situation.** Ask questions. Instead of trying to expose weaknesses (Sharon's *modus operandi*), look for strengths. You can note the negatives, but don't dwell on them; instead try to uncover what is underneath, what the other person is really searching for. You may find that your assumptions are wrong and that the conflict is resolved merely by listening to the other person's wants and needs. If nothing else, you may at least agree to disagree.

3. **Have a game plan if attacked or provoked.** Decide how you want to handle a volatile situation under anger or duress before it happens. And most importantly, decide how much effort you want to give to this situation. It may be worth ignoring the provocation. The person may not mean enough to you to go through all of the agony you must go through to work through a problem.

4. **Spend your time and energy wisely.** Mentally rehearse what you are going to say. Write it down and practice with someone you trust. There is learning that takes place in the practice. It is much better to make mistakes and refine your technique with a friend than to flounder when you are in the emotional heat of the moment. Feedback from your practice will also help to ensure that you use the right words and tone. It is easy to judge and let critical words creep into our dialogue when there is repressed anger. It is much better to be truthful, but to express your truth with respect.

Techniques You Can Use in Conflict Situations

➤ Ignore it.

➤ Stay positive. Take the "high road." Even when provoked, stay positive.

➤ Reframe their attacks. "You were saying what?" Ask for clarification.

➤ Use the "Columbo Effect." Play dumb and ask a lot of questions.

➤ Speak your truth. Recognize the truth of what is happening and say it out loud.

➤ Assert dominance. Match them with power and dominance. Assert that you are the "leader of the pack."

Explanation of the Techniques

Ignore it. This is self-explanatory. Do this if you decide that it isn't worth the time and energy you would have to put into resolving the conflict.

Stay positive. This involves taking the "high road" on every response, almost as if you don't understand the other person's anger or need to get to you. Stay above the fray. This is difficult to do and requires you to be balanced and centered before you have interactions with this person. It will be explained in further detail in the chapter on "Balance and Centering," but it is important to note that your thoughts and mental imagery are helpful to your success with this technique.

I have found it useful to say a prayer for protection before facing someone I know is going to be negative with me.

> *Dear God. In a few minutes I'm going to be face to face with someone who causes me a great deal of (pain, hurt, fear, conflict, etc.). I ask that you give me a greater understanding of them and guide me to know what to say and how to say the*

words that will ease this tension between us. Please protect me and keep me safe from harm. I pray for courage and will relax with the strength of your love and protection by my side.

If you are in tune with yourself, you will know what protection you need and what to ask for. Sometimes I ask for angels or guides to help me through. Sometimes I seek understanding with humor. I use visual imagery and pretend that I'm putting on an astronaut suit or that I'm surrounded by a large white force field from *Star Wars*. The mental imagery and fun help me to not be so vulnerable to their attacks, and I find that our interactions are quite different than if I was not prepared in this way.

Reframe. This involves restating what the person said in an attempt to make sure you have understood her completely. It is as if you are a journalist and clarifying details in order to get the story right. "Just the facts, ma'am."

A coaching client of mine had a problem with an uncooperative employee. She was the owner of a medical office and was concerned about quality of service and sterilization procedures. One of her employees was not as conscientious as the owner would have liked and did not operate as a team player. When crunch times came at the beginning or end of the day, the employee would complain and was not willing to do more than was in her job description. The owner would get impatient with the employee's attitude and lose her cool in dealing with the employee. We explored many techniques, but the owner found reframing to work best for her in the moment of conflict. In this example, the owner is a King, and Julie the employee is a Storyteller.

Owner: "We're getting really busy. Julie, please sterilize those instruments and see if Amy needs any help."

Julie: (Mumbles something under her breath) "I've got to finish counting inventory for the order that goes out today."

Owner: (Thinks: Here she goes again, making things hard for me. Can't she see that we are swamped and taking care of clients is more important than getting out the order?) "Julie, are you saying that you need to do the order first before you can help Amy with the clients?"

Julie: (Thinks: What a pain. I wanted to meet a friend after work and now it looks as if I'm going to be late if I wait to do the order.) "I'd like to finish the order first."

Owner: (Thinks: Unbelievable!) "You'd like to finish the order first?"

Julie: "Yeah."

Owner: (Thinks: Okay, take a deep breath and remember to reframe—state how her behavior impacts the office and ask what she will do about it.) "If you finish the order first, instead of helping Amy, it will take an extra hour to treat the five people in the waiting room. The staff will have to work at least an hour late, and we've all worked ten hours already. I don't want to do that, and neither do the other assistants. What do you think is a better suggestion for all of us to get out on time?"

Julie: (Thinks: I'm boxed in. I wanted to leave on time, too.) "Okay, I see your point. I'll help Amy, but I want everyone to pitch in and give me their inventory figures instead of me counting them so I can finish the order faster."

My client said she felt a tremendous sense of accomplishment that she was able to confront and get her point across to this employee without losing her temper. The owner said that normally she wouldn't have said anything; she would have gone home, overworked and frustrated, and complained to her close friends instead of dealing directly with the issue. By reframing and respectfully confronting her employee, the owner empowered herself. Then, by asking for a plan of action, she empowered her employee by engaging her in the process.

Reframing is a great technique for changing the energy flow of a situation as well as gaining understanding of a situation. An additional benefit: If the other person is not well-intentioned, she usually becomes exacerbated and gives up or will soften in time.

Use the Columbo Effect. Taken from an old television series, this technique involves dancing around the issue, playing dumb so to speak, doggedly pursuing your purpose. It throws the negative person off her game. It appears to the other person as if you are fumbling and bumbling and may not even be a worthy adversary. This technique can be quite powerful because you are in control of your emotions.

I have practiced this successfully over years of dealing with potentially volatile situations. One involved someone in my family who on occasion likes to throw out comments that are meant to be hurtful and inflammatory. Although I may feel anger when this happens, I go through the template listed earlier. I decide that it is worth spending energy on this person, because she is a member of the family. I also know that if I confront directly or speak my truth, it will only make the small situation bigger, so I choose the *Columbo Effect*.

It is possible that this family member thinks that I'm a dimwitted, spineless person. Yet, I've been successfully able to avoid escalating arguments and bad situations by reframing "let me get this straight" and by acting confused or as if I really didn't know what was going on.

An example of a conversation would start with the family member making the opening comment, "Ashley said she was upset with you about not calling her last week. You were in town, and you didn't even think to call your sister."

The gauntlet is thrown. I have many choices. I could respond in anger, because I felt that it is none of her business and because if Ashley was angry, she could call me herself. I could respond with how I truly feel, or I could confront her. I could also feel guilty because I didn't call Ashley. The choice is up to me.

151

From experience, I knew the phone call wasn't about Ashley; it was about power and control. Any attempts to dislodge that control would result in me getting dragged into a long, unpleasant conversation that would leave me feeling drained. So instead I opt for, "Geez, hard to believe, I had no idea Ashley was in town."

Then my family member responds with a stronger, more forceful attempt at getting to me. "I guess you're too busy to bother with your family. I thought family was more important to you than that. You always seem to have the time to do the things you want to do." Then, silence.

I know the first person to respond is a goner, so I don't say anything. After a while, the family member says, "Well, you certainly don't seem to be talkative today so I guess we'll have to get off the phone."

My response, "Gee, thanks for calling. What is it that you wanted to tell me?"

Her response, "Oh nothing. You seem to be busy, I'm just bothering you."

I say, "Thanks, hope to talk to you again soon. Bye." Click.

I accomplished my mission of staying positive, not getting dragged into a manipulative game.

Speak your truth. When confronted with someone attacking you or not giving you what you want, tell the person truthfully how you feel. This can be accomplished in a positive, loving way. It is enough to say, "I'm feeling uncomfortable with your comments and would appreciate it if you would stop talking about me/her/him/it that way."

Sometimes people are unaware of how they are coming across to others and need a wake-up call. They may simply need someone to say, "Hey, this is what you sound like, and I don't like it."

State what you need to say in clear, objective terms. Then be truthful about your feelings. To do this, it is important to have completed the first step: know yourself. If possible, explain what effect the other person's behavior has had on you or the given situation and ask for her to let you know what she is going to do about it. In this way, you are putting the ownership back in her court and are asking her to accept responsibility for her actions. You are also seeking closure, and if she is not able to do so, at least it will be clear where you stand with her. Let's look at how this works.

Sheila, a Warrior, was playing doubles with a partner, Jessica, also a Warrior. Jessica was notorious for having a bad attitude on the tennis court. They were playing a smart doubles team that played together regularly. Since Sheila and Jessica had only played together a few times, Jessica did not know Sheila's playing style well. Jessica was beginning to doubt Sheila's competence because they did not win their last match. To Jessica, playing well meant winning. To Sheila, playing well meant playing with integrity, to the best of her ability, and having a good time.

They started out okay, but at 2–2 in the first set, Sheila hit her first overhead into the net. Jessica shot her an "Oh, no" look, and Sheila's confidence dived. During the same game, Sheila hit two more overheads into the net. Sheila thought her partner was going to take her head off. She typically hit her overheads well and was just as frustrated as Jessica. Jessica huffed and sighed and finally went over to Sheila and said, "Let it bounce next time. Whatever you do, don't take it in the air!"

After that reprimand, Sheila couldn't play. She tried to do what Jessica said, but her confidence sank further and she forgot everything she knew about the game. Sheila was practically useless on the court. What Sheila really needed was for Jessica to say, "Shake it off. You know what to do, so let's get out there and do it together." She needed for Jessica to step up to the plate, force some points, and give her time to get her confidence back. Sheila needed for Jessica to work with her as a team.

Instead, Jessica began to yell at Sheila on the court. She was livid and most likely embarrassed because they were receiving quite a thrashing. At the changeover, after losing the first set, Sheila summoned up the courage to respond to her partner. In Warrior-like fashion, she pulled Jessica aside and said to her, "Listen, I don't care what you think about me off the court, but as long as we're playing together on this court, I want you to believe in me. If you don't, we might as well concede the match, because we've already lost. I can't play with you, if you don't believe we can win this together." Sheila said this with a firm voice and a no-nonsense look in her eye. Probably no one had ever talked to Jessica that way before. She didn't say anything, but Sheila did sense a change in her attitude. They finished the match with some semblance of unity.

The outcome wasn't the stuff of fairy tales. They lost the match, and Jessica abruptly stormed off the court without shaking Sheila's hand or anyone else's (the ultimate rudeness in tennis). Sheila had the distinct impression that Jessica called their captain later that day and asked that she never be teamed with Sheila again. Although several of Sheila's team members called Sheila to apologize for Jessica's behavior, none of them had ever spoken to the woman about her superior attitude. She was simply allowed to bully her way into what she wanted.

By matching Jessica's Warrior behavior, in a clear, nonjudgmental way, Sheila was able to get Jessica to listen and then was able to lead her to behavior that enabled them to at least finish the match. This happens so often in our daily lives. We cannot control other people, only our own behavior and reactions. It is important to remember that if we want something to change, at first we need to take a look at what we can change within our own behavior in order to get the desired impact. Sometimes the only benefit is that we are left with our self-esteem intact.

Assert dominance. At times, some people can become so adversarial that they aren't able to listen to calmness and will only listen when someone first stands up to them. Then they back down and are able to listen.

These people only respect power. They enter relationships seeking control and back down only when they are forced to. There are times when these people are best dealt with using the "Leader of the Pack" technique. Much as dogs and wolves do, there is always a leader, one who exerts authority over others in the pack. In the pack, the leader asserts his or her dominance by physically standing over the offending pack member, thereby conveying the message: "I am in control. I am more powerful. I am the authority, so what I say goes."

Sometimes in our day-to-day relationships, we encounter a situation that calls for us to use the knowledge of the "Leader of the Pack." For example, if someone is shouting insults at you and you are being backed into a corner, you could remain positive or reframe what they're saying, but it could only serve to make them angrier. They may feel placated and patronized even though your intentions are merely to diffuse an ugly situation with the most dignity you can muster.

Someone who is negative and absorbed with her own power will only respect you after you assert power or dominance over her. When someone is that far gone into her anger, sometimes yelling back at the person jars her out of her angry altered state and clears the air enough for her to calm down. It is almost as if you've allowed the person to blow off steam, but set the boundary by growling, "All right, enough is enough!"

The power of the situation has shifted to you, but instead of abusing it as the angry person did, breathe deeply, let your anger pass, and in silence allow her the space to save face. Later, when the anger is gone, is the time to further address the issue if needed. Keep in mind that the offending party may feel embarrassed by her outburst and you may have to be the one to clear the air so you can get past where you are to a resolution.

By remaining calm yet calling her bluff, so to speak, you are choosing how you will respond. You have the freedom to act instead of react. And that, in itself, is extremely empowering.

People who have a need to dominate respect power and will respond better when they are placed into a situation that forces them to recognize your power. It is strange, but sometimes the best way to deal with someone who is verbally abusing you is to match her where she is. You respond to her with the same verbal intensity, the same tone, the same degree of loudness then lead her to a different way of behavior. This technique is called *matching and pacing* and is based on the premise that it is easier to lead someone when you are speaking her language.

Keep in mind that this is not the scenario of choice. It would be better to resolve conflicts in a more positive, civilized manner. But when confronted with an overbearing personality, it will not suffice to placate her or stay positive. Such people are not ready to listen yet.

Take the example of two friends: Kathy (Warrior-King) tends to be overbearing and blames others for problems, while Sara (Artisan-Server) tends to acquiesce and blame herself for things that go wrong. Their friendship has survived because Sara is the giver, the one who listens and is there to pick up the pieces for her friend Kathy. Finally, Kathy takes advantage of Sara one too many times. Kathy abusively yells at Sara and demeans her without thinking of Sara's feelings.

Kathy: "What a day! I can hardly believe what Julie said about me. She actually thinks I stabbed her in the back! She ran me down in front of everybody. She's a gossip and a bitch!"

Sara: "Oh, I can't believe Julie would do something like that. She always seems so nice."

Kathy: "Nice? What do you call nice? She's a pig. Look at her. She needs to lose about fifteen pounds. And look at the way she dresses. I think she buys her clothes from Goodwill."

Sara: "Surely you don't mean that. You know she doesn't have a lot of money for extra things because she's paying for night school to get a better job. Besides, what do her clothes have to do with her being nice. And what does that have to do with you?"

Kathy: "No offense, Sara, but what planet are you on? It has everything to do with her being jealous of me so much that she'd run me down in front of the boss and the rest of the office. It has everything to do with impressing some guy she's so desperate to go out with."

Sara: "Kathy, I think you're making a bigger deal out of this than you mean to..."

Kathy: Interrupts. "What! Are you siding with her? What kind of friend are you anyway? I thought you cared about me. How could you defend her?"

The words were out of her mouth before she could take them back and they had their desired effect. Sara was devastated and countered after a few moments of reflection.

Sara: Answering with a raised voice, "I can because you're wrong. You don't deserve a friend like me. I see you for how you really are: selfish, frustrated, and unhappy, and I'm still your friend. How can I defend a person like Julie when you unjustifiably blame her for your insecurities and problems? I can. I do. And I will."

Silence.

It took some time for Kathy to calm down. She was angry, embarrassed, and unsure of what to say.

Sara asserted her authority over Kathy and did it in a positive, affirming way. She spoke the truth about what Kathy was saying. She said, "Enough is enough." She tried to tell Kathy first in a nonthreatening gentle way and when Kathy didn't respond, she was forced to get Kathy to back down with harsher words. Painful as it was for Kathy to hear, it would have been more painful for Sara to let her continue. Kathy has a true friend with Sara. One who will tell her the truth and be willing to help her work through problems and tough situations.

How to End Confrontations on a Positive Note

Always try to leave interactions with another person (even if only in your mind) on a positive note. This keeps your energy and thoughts heading towards a higher purpose instead of getting bogged down with mundane, energy-draining issues such as, "Why is this happening to me?" "I really can't stand that person," "I wish they'd go away," "If only they weren't in my life, everything would be so much better." Staying positive leads to the best possible outcome for both of you.

One way of staying positive is to share your positive feelings with other people. In his book *The Biology of Success*, Bob Arnot describes this as "emotional broadcasting." He says that sharing positive thoughts helps to unlock an emotional response in the listener. The listener then responds in kind with positive feedback. Positive feeds on positive, and a cycle is created. The result is that you *both* feel better. To do this effectively, Arnot says you need to follow a few basic steps:

➤ **Train your emotions.** Act the way you want to feel and your emotions will follow. Arnot says to act the way you want to feel. In other words, act like the response you want and eventually you will train yourself to feel that way.

➤ **Use positive affirmations.** A key to this success is self-talk. Use positive affirmations and positive voices when you are thinking. Sports psychologists and athletes have long known that this is an integral part of their success. Using affirmations can help change a belief system and help someone transcend performance. In short, train the mind and the muscles will follow.

➤ **Build a network.** You are not an island and do not stand alone. Surround yourself with success. Develop relationships in which you can give and receive emotional support.

➤ **Don't play God or psychologist.** Avoid the "Pygmalion" syndrome. Your positivity can influence others, but there is no guarantee. Odds are if you are being positive out of your own ego with an expectation that others will change to benefit you, it won't happen and you'll wind up doing more harm than good. The positive energy you put out has to be without expectation that the other person will change. When you're not asking for it, it may just happen.

➤ **Stay away from idle gossip about that person or anyone for that matter.** It doesn't do them or you any good. Notice how you feel when you're gossiping about someone else. It drags you down to a lower level and sets up a domino of negative energy that is heading in the opposite direction from the positive changes women want to bring about.

Big Hearts

Give us big hearts, dear God;
big enough to embrace all our sisters
and brothers
especially those in trouble,
whether of their own making or
because of wrongs done to them.
Give us big hearts, dear God;
big enough to acknowledge our own weakness
before pointing the finger at others;
big enough to be humble
when blessed with your good gifts
denied to so many.
Give us big hearts, dear God;
to reach out again and again
to those who cannot help themselves
until hope is restored to them
and we, thorn-beaten and bloodied
allow our loving to become more like yours.

KATHY KEAY
Laughter, Silence and Shouting:
An Anthology of Women's Prayers

Conflict on a Large Scale

Sometimes the conflict is larger. It may be a family; a neighborhood; a department at work; an entire religion, culture, or country. Whatever the differences, resolution can start by identifying where you are, where the other person is, and where you want to go. When the problem is larger scale, it may seem impossible to resolve. It may seem that one person can't do anything, but one can. The change can start from within; even if it seems small, it will lead to changes in others. One can feel overwhelmed and defeated when faced with the enormity of a large problem. Instead of getting stuck in thoughts of helplessness, remember that you can only control yourself. You can't control others, but you can affect change in others by changing yourself first.

If you are stuck and not sure how to proceed with a conflict, it may help to get quiet and look deep inside yourself to get the answers from within. I believe that each of us is born with a sort of self-guidance system. If we turn toward our intuitive guides, they will help steer us in the right direction, the direction to help us be the better part of who we are. The answers lie within.

To access this intuition, we must practice and spend time alone with ourselves in silence. We must learn to listen instead of talk. One way to learn this is through meditation. Yet some people find it difficult to meditate without a goal; it is agonizing for them to just sit and be still. We can ease our way into this silence using a technique called *guided imagery*. In chapter 2, we used a guided imagery to help us come in contact with our higher self, or inner voice. Now we will utilize the same technique to help us resolve conflicts.

EXERCISE

Guided Imagery for Conflict Resolution

As before, you may wish to record this guided imagery on tape so that you won't have to be disturbed reading the text. It is also a good idea to have a journal or paper handy to write down information you gather during the exercise.

Before you start, have a good mental image of the conflict you wish to resolve. The conflict may be with a boss, coworker, neighbor, spouse, or friend. Assess your feelings. How much of your energy do you want to put into resolving this conflict? If you don't know, then that may be a good starting point for the guided imagery.

Find a comfortable position. You can sit on a chair with your feet flat on the floor, or lie down with all of your body in a relaxed position. Eventually you may be able to do these exercises sitting cross-legged on the floor or in some other posture. It is important that your body be free from tension, and it may be difficult to assume a relaxed state in a more complex posture. Your body can hold tension even when you are not aware of it. For instance, when you hold your breath, your body is holding tension in the diaphragm, the muscles around the lungs, the connecting muscles up to the neck and shoulders, etc. So it is important to relax all of the muscles of the body and to keep the breath going. Breath is the means by which our body clears the muscles from tension and re-oxygenates the blood.

Before you begin, offer a prayer for protection. Here is one I often use:

God, I ask for your protection and guidance in helping me to resolve the problem I set before you today. Within your will and for my highest good, I ask that any and all negativity be removed from me. I ask to be surrounded by Christ, my guides, angels, and protectors and for this blessing I give thanks.

After saying this prayer or one of your own, continue to breathe deeply to relax your body. Now let's begin the guided imagery.

Imagine that you are lying in a sunny place—perhaps the beach or a secluded meadow. Your arms and legs are re-laxed. There is no tension in your body. Imagine the warmth of the sun is a golden ball that starts at your feet. The golden ball warms your toes and insteps. In a circular motion it glides up your legs, relaxing and melting all tension as it goes. Up the ankles, the calves, the knees, it pulses and warms the muscles, relaxing as it moves. Up the thighs, into your but-tocks, across your abdomen, glowing and warming as it moves along. As it pulses in your abdomen, you feel the warmth in your lower back at the base of your spine. The heat builds as it pulses and glows. You feel the warmth and energy rise up the back of your spine as mercury rises in a thermometer. Slowly the warmth spreads from your spine and abdomen to your chest and all of the muscles surrounding your lungs. You feel heavy and peaceful as the golden warmth spreads to your neck and shoulders. Allow the ball to pulse at your shoul-ders for a few moments to relax the extra tension you hold there. Then let your shoulders drop and melt under its warmth.

Let your jaw drop, your mouth fall open and breathe deeply. The warmth is now relaxing any tension from your jaw and the muscles in your face. Relax your cheeks, the muscles around your eyes, your eyebrows. Let them fall into deep relaxation. Relax the muscles in your forehead and let the warmth of the golden ball continue to your scalp. As it rises above your head, your body is completely relaxed and glowing.

Imagine you are going on a long journey. You travel to a special place, a place where you feel safe and comfortable. (I imagine myself in a large, lit, warm room deep in the earth in a cave. I am warm and protected and cocooned. It feels safe and sacred to me.) It need not be a place with a name or a place that really exists. It only needs to feel safe and familiar to you.

After you reach your safe place, have a seat and ask that all of the special guidance you requested during your prayer for protection be available to you in this place. When you feel safe and empowered by the protection around you, ask for the image of the person with whom you wish to resolve the conflict with to appear. Keep this image at a distance until you feel comfortable with it. Note the image. What does it look like? Does it look exactly like the person in real life? Or does it look different? How do you feel with this image in your sacred place? Does it feel threatening to you? Do you feel scared? Content? Angry? Attacked? For a moment, allow the energy from this image to be in this place with you.

After a moment, decide what you want to say to this person. This is the time to decide how much energy you want to put into resolving the conflict. If at this point you decide there is no hope for resolution because this person harbors too much animosity towards you or this person doesn't mean enough to you to spend any more time on her, then simply thank her for her time and say good-bye. If you decide to continue, then let this person know why you wanted to talk to her.

You can lay out the whole problem in detail or simply state

that you wanted to resolve the conflict between you and let the person start the talking. Your communication may be in thoughts, words, or feelings. The person may move or show you images to convey what she wants to tell you. Listen and show her the respect that you would wish to be shown.

If the person doesn't say anything, start with your feelings, with what you would like to see to resolve your conflict. Let the person respond. She will tell you what you need to know. If there is no response, that tells you something. If she indicates that you have to do all the changing, that tells you that she isn't willing to work at a resolution. Again if she isn't willing to work, simply acknowledge her time, let her see your image of a resolution, and send her on her way. If you plant the seed, it may take root.

In the best course of things, the person will be responsive to working towards a resolution. Listen carefully to what she says and see if it is congruent with what she says and how she acts in real life. Many times people are reluctant to show their true feelings and create elaborate masks behind which to hide. This imagery process will enable you to see through the mask and will guide you to who they really are. You may find your own resistance melting away when you see the other person's truth. It may not change what you do, but it will certainly help you to be able to empathize with her. This alone is enough to change your relationship.

After you've explained your side of the story and have listened to the other person tell you her viewpoint, ask her what *she wants from you*. Listen and decide if you can give this to her. Tell her. Then let her know what *you want from her*. Listen for her response. If she says she can give that to you, thank her. If not, tell her that is what you need.

You may use the remaining time together to work through any other unresolved issues. Ask questions. Say whatever you wish to say. After you are finished, imagine a giant, warm, white cocooning light surrounding both of you, protecting you and elevating you to the highest level of thought and communication. If you feel comfortable, give the other person a hug, thank her, and say good-bye. Release her so that you are not tied to her after you finish the exercise. Imagine her disappearing or walking away so that you are alone in your sacred place.

Spend a few moments reflecting on what transpired. Take note of how you feel. Are you relaxed? Content? Sad? Relieved? Do you have a sense of completion? Or do you have unfinished business? Be still in the silence.

Then slowly, ever so slowly, begin to bring yourself back into consciousness. Thank God and your guides and protectors for their help and begin to feel your body. Be aware of your hands and feet, arms and legs, your heartbeat, the blinking of your eyelids. Be conscious of your breath and allow yourself to be aware of your surroundings. Hear the sounds in the room. You may open your eyes.

Before you go on to another task, take a few moments to write what transpired in your sacred place. Write what happened when you made contact with the other person. What words were spoken? Were there any images? Everything may be clear now but in a few hours or days it may be forgotten, so it is important to take the time right after an imagery or meditation to write the details. This is also a way of honoring the information you glean from the imagery so that in the future your subconscious will trust that this is important and be willing to work deeper and easier when you ask it to.

Chapter Summary

In this chapter, we learned:

➤ There are ways of dealing with conflict proactively rather than reactively.

➤ Seek to understand the conflict. Use the Seven Aspects to help.

➤ How to deal with negative people.

➤ How to use our own power to create a positive environment for conflict resolution.

CHAPTER SIX

BEING CENTERED AND FINDING YOUR BALANCE

Happiness is inward, and not outward, and so it does not depend on what we have, but on what we are.

Henry Van Dyke

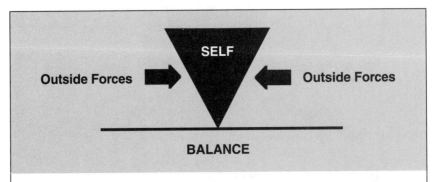

Achieving balance may be thought of as an upside-down triangle, seeking equilibrium at a single point. Our lives are much like that. Balance can be achieved at a single point in time. We need to remember how it feels, because forces in our lives throw us out of balance. Whether family, friends, work, health, or our emotions, our lives are not static; they are dynamic.

The knowingness that comes from remembering the balance is our center. We can always go back to it, and recreate that feeling if we keep it anchored in our consciousness.

TO KEEP ONE'S CENTER in the midst of the ever-quickening pace of life is important. This is an essential ingredient to maintaining integrity in your relationships. It is difficult to stay in alignment with your values if you allow yourself to be pulled off center in other directions at the whim of the emotions and energies of the people around you.

Finding your center helps you find the sacredness in all things. It lessens the drama and pain of life around us and helps us to cope. It is a critical skill to acquire in order to survive our world today. If the stress and pace of today's societies don't get you psychologically, they will sabotage your physical body through sickness and all forms of aches and pain. Eventually, stress will kill you.

Satellites and the Internet have created a world of instantaneous communication. We observed the celebration of the millennium across all time zones of the planet. We witnessed the ravages of war in Bosnia and Desert Storm. We watch the French Open in South America while it is being played in Paris and thrill to live coverage of the Olympics. By the touch of a keyboard, we can communicate within a second to someone on the other side of the world. Technology has compressed our time-space continuum. It has accelerated everything that is going on in our world today. Communication. Business. Drama. Sports. Tension. Change. Stress.

Our bodies are not meant to live in a constant adrenaline rush. The flight or fight syndrome served us well in primitive societies, but in the sophisticated playing field of today's world, it only serves to break us down. Confronted with stress, our adrenal system secretes hormones to send messages to critical parts of our brain and nervous system to be on alert. "This is it! The big time! Ready for battle! Man your stations!" The various muscles and organs in our body influenced by these hormones are stimulated for immediate use. When this stress is constant, our systems become overtaxed and worn-out. Large quantities of rest are needed to counteract the damage caused by circuit overload. Rest can be achieved in the midst of this call to action on the adrenal system by "detaching" and staying in one's center.

How can you stay centered? It is easy to be centered and calm when walking alone on a mountain trail with no one around. The rhythm of your footsteps keeps cadence with the natural sounds around you. You feel expanded and your senses are heightened. Smells are more pungent, colors are more vibrant, and sounds are clearer, as if you are experiencing everything on a higher plane, in a way you've never experienced them before.

That awareness comes from being centered. Some people accomplish this through meditation or prayer. Some through breathwork, exercise, or diet. There are also people who achieve this through reading and intellectual understanding.

There are many things we can do to be centered and find our balance.

The real art is learning what works for each of us. Here are a few suggestions:

1. Maintain a positive self-image.

2. Learn the art of saying NO.

3. Take care of your body through diet, sleep, and exercise.

4. Take care of yourself by being your own best friend. Surround yourself with people who nurture you rather than put you down.

5. Learn relaxation techniques and practice them.

6. Give up the need to be right. Stay centered and "detached" from the chaos around you.

7. Have faith in a higher power.

8. Laugh, play more, and have a sense of humor.

9. Develop a personal life vision.

10. Spend time in silence every day, meditate, pray.

11. Give time and energy to others. Volunteer.

12. Rekindle a sense of place and reconnect with nature.

13. Develop a sense of community.

14. Teach and mentor what you know and are learning.

15. Live your life with integrity and from the heart.

Maintain a Positive Self-image

Having a positive self-image creates a healthy mind-body relationship. In other words, "you really are what you think." Many women play the game of turning gold into garbage by discounting compliments. Continually doing so embeds the negative comments into your consciousness where they are eventually made real by your body that believes them. We can cancel those thoughts by simply saying, "Cancel that thought," or by reframing the negative thought in a positive way.

Negative thoughts are like debts—they drain or take away from our energy reserves. Holding on to them increases the drain and takes away from our physical and emotional vitality. Eventually, we have to pay back the debt by replacing the energy. One of the most significant ways of replacing/releasing the energy is to let go of negative thought patterns.

For example, the thought "I could just kill her when she does that" could be changed to "I would really like it if she would include me in on the conversation instead of excluding me." Because you really don't want to "kill her"; you just want her to treat you differently. Our self-directed dialogues are also important to change. If we beat ourselves up by saying, "I am so stupid; how could I have ever made that mistake?" you can be sure that you will not only make that mistake again, but that you will be perceived as incompetent by others. A more effective thought would be to say, "Wait a minute! Cancel that thought! I'm human. I made a mistake. Now I know what to do. Next time I'll proofread the letter more carefully and even have someone else proof it before I send it off." That is a more effective thought and leaves you with a positive (empowering) self-image rather than a negative one that will only beat your mind and body down.

EXERCISE

Collecting Gold

What might happen if you were to devote the next three days to listening and looking for the "strokes" or positive comments aimed in your direction?

What if you were to accept them with nothing more than a simple "thank you"? Here are some of the experiences you might notice:

- The thank you's of a bus driver
- The admiring looks of your children
- The comment of a coworker, a client, a student, a customer
- The comment of a teacher or a coach
- A stray dog following you home
- An obliging motorist who stops to let you through the traffic
- A wink, a whistle, a second look
- An acquaintance remembering your name
- A letter from home
- A phone call from a friend
- A hug and a kiss
- A discount, a bargain, a dime in the pay phone
- A grateful waiter
- Your newspaper left in a plastic bag on a rainy day
- A luncheon date
- A sunset more dramatic than any you can remember
- A cool evening, a warm fire, a feeling of well-being

Why not try it and make up your own list. You may even find that you have written a poem.[1]

Learn the Art of Saying NO

Most women have a difficult time being assertive enough to take care of themselves. While they may be capable of asserting themselves at work, when they come home they melt into doormats. Or conversely, they may be able to hold the line at home, but when it comes to work or to volunteer activities, they are afraid to let someone down. They may even be afraid that people will think less of them if they don't do what was asked. Being assertive basically means that you are able to clearly express your thoughts and wishes and, at the same time, are able to keep the lines of communication open with the other person.

Many women were taught not to say *no* as a child. They were taught to give the responsibility of judging what they should and should not do to someone else.

This leads to the stereotypical female behavior of asking a question that the woman already knows the answer to: "Honey, what do you think of this dress? Does the color look good on me?" Or "My feelings were hurt by what Jill said to me the other day. Should I tell her how I feel?" Or "Do you think I should be in charge of that committee again this year?" She already knows the answers to her questions, "Yes, the dress looks great. How much do you value Jill's friendship? And NO you should not chair the committee again this year." Yet she has a difficult time deciding for herself, because she was taught that other people know better about these things than she does. Over and over, she has been told:

"Just swallow your pride."

"How could you say such a thing?"

"You wouldn't want to give the impression you really felt that way, would you?"

"It is not very lady-like to throw a temper tantrum!"

The poem, "Angela's Word," illustrates this point clearly.

173

Angela's Word

When Angela was very young,
Age two or three or so,
Her mother and her father
Taught her never to say NO.
They taught her that she must agree
With everything they said,
And if she didn't, she was spanked
And sent upstairs to bed.

So Angela grew up to be
A most agreeable child;
She was never angry
And she was never wild;
She always shared, she always cared,
She never picked a fight,
And no matter what her Parents said,
She thought that they were right.

Angela the Angel did very well in school
And, as you might imagine, she followed every rule;
Her teachers said she was so well-bred,
So quiet and so good,
But how Angela felt inside
They never understood.

Angela had lots of friends
Who liked her for her smile;
They knew she was the kind of gal
Who'd go the extra mile;
And even when she had a cold
And really needed rest,
When someone asked her if she'd help
She always answered Yes.

When Angela was thirty-three she was a lawyer's wife.
She had a home and family, and a nice suburban life.
She had a little girl of four
And a little boy of nine,
And if someone asked her how she felt
She always answered, "Fine."

But one cold night near Christmastime
When her family was in bed,
She lay awake as awful thoughts
went spinning through her head;
She didn't know why, and she didn't know how,
But she wanted her life to end;
So she begged Whoever put her here
To take her back again.

And then she heard, from deep inside,
A voice that was soft and low;
It only said a single word
And the word it said was...NO.

From that moment on, Angela knew
Exactly what she had to do.
Her life depended on that word,
So this is what her loved ones heard:

NO, I just don't want to;
NO, I don't agree;
NO, that's yours to handle;
NO, that's wrong for me;
NO, I wanted something else;
NO, that hurt a lot!
NO, I'm tired and NO, I'm busy,
And NO, I'd rather not!

Well, her family found it shocking,
Her friends reacted with surprise;
But Angela was different, you could see it in her eyes;
For they've held no meek submission
Since that night three years ago
When Angela the Angel
Got permission to say NO.

Today Angela's a person first, then a mother and a wife.
She knows where she begins and ends,
She has a separate life.
She has talents and ambitions,
She has feelings, needs and goals.
She has money in the bank and
An opinion at the polls.

And to her boy and girl she says,
"it's nice when we agree;
But if you can't say NO, you'll never grow
To be all you're meant to be.
Because I know I'm sometimes wrong
And because I love you so,
You'll always be my angels
Even when you tell me NO."[2]

BARABARA K. BASSETT
Chicken Soup for the Woman's Soul

Take Care of Yourself Through Proper Diet, Sleep, and Exercise

Are you a Type A woman? Are you someone who multitasks to the exponential level? Mention Type A behavior and the most common image that springs to mind is that of the harried *male* business executive. But according to a study published by Dr. Meyer Friedman and Dr. Roy Rosenman in 1974, women are not immune to Type A behavior or to developing heart disease. Typically women are more likely to suffer congestive heart failure or angina rather than to dramatically drop dead from a heart attack.

Friedman discovered that Type A women were seven times more likely than Type B women to develop heart disease.[3] In a related study, the Framingham Heart Study, Type A women showed four times the heart disease risk of men.[4]

The hallmarks of Type A behavior are time urgency, relentless drive for achievement, the inability to relax, and a free-floating hostility that may be expressed less directly in women than in men. In an article in the *Medical Self-Care* magazine, writer Michael Castleman quoted Diane Ulmer, a writer and Type A head nurse of the emergency room of a leading medical center, as saying, "My biggest Type A problems were a time urgency and overscheduling. I was always terribly impatient with myself and with everyone else. I spoke very quickly, interrupted people, and was always in a rush. I also had trouble delegating. Rather than trusting someone else with a task, I'd take it upon myself, which gave me even more to do."[5]

Friedman and Ulmer, who teamed up in 1984 book, *Treating Type A Behavior and Your Heart*, maintain that as women move into jobs historically held by men, they find it difficult to find a balance between their personal and work lives. "Fired up to beat men at their own game, many Type A women work fifty- to sixty-hour weeks. In addition, they shop and cook for themselves, their children, husbands, or boyfriends; do their housekeeping, laundry, and ironing; attend exercise classes; [run their children to various activities]; see friends; and try to appear attractive and feminine at all times."[6]

Women are faced with contradicting forces. They take care of the family, take care of work and take care of themselves. The pressure is tripled, and many women feel frustrated and angry. But since they were taught that it is not "feminine" to express anger, they suppress their anger and transform it into depression (anger turned inward) and disease (cancer, heart disease, etc.).

Ulmer offers techniques to help women feel more secure with their emotions, especially anger, and to be more assertive. "Type A women need to learn new ways to recognize and deal with their anger," she says. "They need to find the middle ground of assertive nonaggressive negotiation between swallowing their anger and exploding into temper tantrums."[7] Ulmer practiced on herself and learned that, by adopting more Type B behavior, she could have a longer, peaceful, more fulfilling life. Both Type A and Type B behaviors are illustrated in figure 6.1.

FIGURE 6.1[8]

Characteristics of Type A Women and Things to
Start Doing To Become a Type B

Type A	Aspiring Type B
• Tries to do several things at once: reads while watching TV, cooks while on the phone.	• Listen to your spouse and friends. Stop arguing with suggestions to slow down.
• Eats quickly without savoring food.	• Realize that life is always unfinished. Stop expecting yourself to accomplish everything at once.

FIGURE 6.1

*Characteristics of Type A Women and Things to
Start Doing To Become a Type B*

Type A	Aspiring Type B
• Tends to sit on the edge of her seat, like a runner straining at the starting blocks.	• Look at your schedule and ask yourself which meetings, dates, and events you will care about one year from now—cancel the rest.
• Has a mania for punctuality. Gets irritated if kept waiting for any reason.	• Focus completely on those who speak to you. Listen carefully. Instead of interrupting, breathe deeply. Think before you answer.
• Remarks on the stupidity of other drivers.	• Drive in the right lane and, as cars pass, ignore them. Instead, reflect on your fondest memories.
• Overschedules herself. Her days are whirlwinds.	• Read a long novel far removed from your professional field of interest.
• Interrupts those who speak slowly or have difficulty making a point. In conversations, often seems preoccupied with other thoughts.	• The next time you see someone doing a task more slowly than you could, do not interfere.
• Pushes herself to accomplish, accomplish, accomplish. Has trouble relaxing and doing nothing.	• Write or call an old friend once a week.
• Has often been told by spouse or friends to slow down. Dismisses these exhortations as ridiculous or impossible.	• Stand in the longest line at the supermarket and use the time to review your progress toward Type B behavior during the previous week. Laugh at yourself at least once a day.

In addition to taking care of yourself by reducing stress, it is also important to get plenty of sleep (at least seven hours a day, eight hours is optimal), eat right, and get a quality amount of exercise. What all of this means varies with the individual. Of course, if you are under a lot of stress, your body may need more sleep than the average person. And if you are a vegetarian or an endurance athlete, your dietary and exercise requirements will differ. The important thing to remember is that not only are you what you think, you are also "what you eat" and "what you do." In other words, we have the power to create a wonderfully happy, healthy, whole human being. It is an awe-inspiring thought. We are not being dragged along through life by fate; we can create and affect the path we take towards our destiny.

Hundreds of books have been written about nutrition, cooking healthy foods, and dietary requirements. Several good resource materials are listed in the last chapter, here are a few: *The Wellness Workbook,* by John W. Travis, M.D., and Regina Sara Ryan; *Eating Well for Optimum Health: The Essential Guide To Food, Diet and Nutrition*, Andrew Weil, M.D.; About.Com's Online Nutrition Guide (http://nutrition.about.com); and Tufts Health and Nutrition Newsletter (http://www.healthletter.tufts. edu/).

The intent is not to repeat what has previously been written, but to simply remind you of the basics.

Golden Rules of Healthier Eating

1. Eat a variety of whole, natural foods that are rich in fiber, calcium, vitamin A, vitamin C, and complex carbohydrates.

2. Avoid foods that contain too much salt, refined sugar, and cholesterol.

3. Keep the amount of fat in your diet to no more than 30 percent of total calories.

4. Drink plenty of water—eight to ten glasses a day unless you need more due to exercise or excessive sweating.

Our diets and eating habits are out of balance because of our lifestyles. We hurry from place to place, sometimes eating fast food on the run without giving it much thought. This is more common in the United States than other countries, but it is becoming an increasing problem in other countries due to the hectic pace of life. In the *Wellness Workbook,* Travis writes, "We have learned to use food to relieve emotional and physical pain because we have lost touch with ourselves." [9]

Travis goes on to explain that poor eating habits, even in a nation of abundance, is a vicious cycle. The poorer our intake of nourishing foods the more out of balance we become. The more out of balance, the more we rely on artificial stimulants in an attempt to create a new balance point. Caffeine, alcohol, nicotine, and a wide variety of drugs are some of the stimulants used to keep us going. Yet the more we rely on artificial means, the less we are in touch with our bodies and the more health problems we create. Similarly, the more we are out of touch with our bodies, the higher the likelihood that we will overeat. We lose touch with our natural body limits and the ability of the body to find its own balance or point of homeostasis (a state of physiological equilibrium produced by a balance of functions and of chemical compositions within an organism).

Exercise: Just do it!

Much like nutrition, there are many ways to find out information about exercise and fitness. It is wise to have a complete physical examination before embarking on any new exercise program. Additionally, a fitness professional can help you by assessing your current level of fitness in: flexibility, cardiovascular, strength, and nutrition. Most personal trainers and fitness clubs offer this service to their clients.

After determining your level of fitness, you are ready for your plan. The plan needs to be personalized to fit your needs and take into consideration your willpower, level of determination, the time you have available, and your fitness goals.

For years, I was a competitive runner, taught yoga classes, skied, played tennis, and worked out religiously. I knew a tremendous amount about health and nutrition and was self-motivated. My perspective changed after having children. The time available for exercise and proper nutrition began to fade away, and year after year I found myself slowly slipping into inactivity and poor eating habits. My exercise consisted of a tennis match once in a while and a lot of driving. If anyone can ever come up with an exercise program that can be done while driving, they could probably make millions! I found myself stressed and rushing. Most people thought I was in good shape, yet I didn't feel good, and I knew I was out of balance.

I began taking classes that combined yoga techniques with more rigorous strengths moves (called Flexible Strength at my club) and started working with a personal trainer. People, observing the class, were amazed when they saw what we did and those, usually men, who thought it looked easy were suitably chagrined after trying a few exercises.

The point of this type of class was to assist your body in using "stabilizers" to build strength. Through stretching and balance movements, complementary muscles, such as abs and smaller muscle groups in your legs, arms, and back, come into play. These are the muscles that we use every day and are the ones that can become problematic for us as we age. When we bend over to pick up a book off the floor or to tie our shoes and we feel our backs "pop," these are the muscles that are the first to go and the hardest to work. I discovered that even though I'm not in shape to run my most competitive times in a race and may be much slower on the slopes, I am less likely to be injured. I actually have better form and balance in the activities I do.

According to personal trainer Ricky Evans at Sportime Fitness, a Pyramids fitness club in Greensboro, North Carolina, it is important to begin with your personal goals. Determine why you want to exercise in the first place, develop a plan to help achieve your goals, then keep evaluating your plan to ensure it is on track and you are having fun. Having fun is key to sticking with your plan. Except for a few driven souls, most people won't stick with an exercise plan in the long run if they aren't having fun, and they certainly won't hang in there if a plan isn't delivering results. Another important point is that goals vary over time. Once a serious competitive runner, I now work out for fitness and balance. Even though I still prefer an intense workout, I don't work out for as long or as often. It has to be convenient and fit in with the rest of my life.

Fitness Resources

Some places to search for information about exercise and fitness are:

➤ **http://www.ivillage.com** Offers information and advice on fitness and nutrition, message boards, chat, and interactive health tools.

➤ **AOL Women: Wellness.** Once in AOL hit keyword: wellness for information on women's health issues covering diverse topics such as fitness, nutrition, skin care, and self-image.

➤ **AOL Women: Fitness.** Once in AOL hit keyword: fitness for fitness advice, features, resources, and related products, especially for women.

➤ **http://www.bodytrends.com/women** Offers women's health, fitness, and exercise equipment—free weights, treadmills, heart rate monitors, ellipticals—as well as articles on flexibility stretching, strength, and aerobic training.

➤ **http://www.cdc.gov/nccdphp/sgr/women.htm** Provides the Surgeon General's report on the beneficial effects of physical activity on women's health.

➤ **http://www.thriveonline.com** Features articles by women's health experts, message boards, and health assessment tools.

➤ **http://www.aol.com/webcenters/health/fitness.adp** Offers workout tips for the workday. Includes a selection of calculators and quizzes to help you assess your physical fitness and links to top health sites.

➤ **http://www.oxygen.com/topic/health/** A good starting point to find out about issues of health, fitness, diet, and nutrition.

Health and Fitness Books

➤ *Body For Life: 12 Weeks To Mental and Physical Strength*, Bill Phillips and Michael D'Orso (Harper Collins, 1999).

➤ *The Pilates Body: The Ultimate At-Home Guide to Strengthening, Lengthening and Toning Your Body—Without Machines*, Brooke Siler (Bantam Doubleday Dell, 2000).

➤ *Strong Women, Stay Young*, Miriam Nelson, Sandy Wernick, and Wendy Wray (Bantam Doubleday Dell, 2000).

➤ *The Complete Book of Fitness: Mind, Body, Spirit, Fitness* magazine (editor) with Karen Andes.

➤ *The Complete Book of Running For Women: Everything You Need To Know About Training, Nutrition, Injury Prevention, Motivation, Racing and Much, Much More*, Claire Kowachik (Simon & Schuster, 1999).

➤ *The Healthy Kitchen: Recipes for a Better Body, Life and Spirit*, Andrew Weil and Rosie Daley (Knopf, 2002).

If you are already involved in a fitness/exercise regime and want to see better results, keep in mind the following: Overuse injuries are seldom accidents. They are usually brought about by excessive repetitive stress placed repeatedly on the body over a period of time. There

Overuse Warning Signs

1. **Resting Pulse:** Take your pulse before moving or getting out of bed in the morning. A morning pulse that is ten beats per minute higher than usual is often a sign that your body is working harder to overcome an impending sickness.

2. **Loss of Sleep:** Determine how much sleep you usually need to feel rested. A reduction in this amount of 5 percent or more can be significant and can be a precursor to injury.

3. **Nighttime:** Do you wake up several times during the night to get a drink or are unable to sleep through the night? This can result in poor sleep quality. You awake not feeling rested, and it is difficult to sleep because you're overly tired, fatigued, and perhaps dehydrated.

4. **Urine Color:** Dark yellow urine means that you are not getting enough water. Dark urine in the morning can be saying that your body is not recovering from the previous day's workout.

5. **Attitude:** Grumpiness, irritability, cold sores, inability to focus or concentrate, and a tiredness that leaves you weak from your very core can signal that you're overdoing it.

If you're experiencing two of these warning signs, reduce the intensity of your training. If three or more, take a day off; you're probably on the brink of injury. There is a tremendous benefit to rest as well as to exercise.

Take Care of Yourself by Being Your Own Best Friend

In a survey of two thousand men and women nationwide, Nina Sue Koch, assistant professor of health and physical education at Hunter College in New York City, discovered that women who exercised regularly (from a walk to gardening to more serious exercise) had more positive feelings about themselves. Many women, especially "high achievers," are out of love with themselves. The price they pay is depression, back problems, and a lower immunity level leaving them vulnerable to chronic and acute diseases.

A study conducted by the University of Rochester School of Medicine found that our immune functions are stronger when we are happy and generally optimistic. Many women have a difficult time staying happy and being their own best friend because they have been putting themselves down for so long that they've forgotten what it feels like to be respected. This self-deprecation can be mirrored in relationships and serves to perpetuate the cycle of low self-esteem. If you're wondering where you fall on the continuum of loving and despising yourself, take the following test.

EXERCISE

Self-Esteem Assessment [10]

For each of the following statements indicate how true it is using the following scale:

    1 — **Not at all true**

    2 — **Somewhat true**

    3 — **About half true**

    4 — **Mostly true**

    5 — **True**

1.   I wish there was someone who would tell me how to solve my personal problems.   _____

2. I don't question my worth as a person even
    if I think others do.   _____

3. When anyone says nice things about me,
    I find it hard to believe. I think they just
    aren't being sincere.   _____

4. When anyone criticizes me, I feel like crying
    or hiding.   _____

5. I don't talk much at parties. I'm afraid
    people will criticize me or laugh at me if
    I say the wrong thing.   _____

6. I'm not living very effectively, but I doubt
    I've got what it takes to do it better.   _____

7. I wish I could change the way I look.   _____

8. Something inside me just won't let me be
    satisfied with any job I've done—if it turns
    out well, I get a smug feeling that the job
    was easy or that I shouldn't be satisfied.   _____

9. I feel different from others and suspect they
    find me physically unattractive.   _____

10. If people I like find out what I'm really like,
    they'll be disappointed in me.   _____

11. I don't like the way I look undressed.   _____

12. I'm shy and self-conscious in social
    situations.   _____

13. To get along and be liked, I tend to do
    what people expect.   _____

14. I have inner strength and self-confidence in
    handling life. I think I'm on solid ground.   _____

15. I feel self-conscious when I'm with people
    who have better jobs or a better education.   _____

16. It's hard to make new friends. I'm so afraid
    they won't like me.   _____

17. I can't help feeling guilty about the way I feel or act towards certain people in my life. _____

18. I only believe in myself about half of the time. _____

19. I'm sensitive to things people say because it sounds as though they're criticizing or insulting me. _____

20. I think I have ability and others say so, but maybe I'm exaggerating. _____

21. I'm confident I can do something about any problem that comes up in the future. _____

22. Sometimes I put on a show to impress others, then I feel ashamed that I'm not the person I pretend to be. _____

23. I don't condemn myself if other people criticize me. That's life. _____

24. I should lose ten pounds. Clothes never look right on me. _____

25. I try to avoid facing a lot of my problems and that makes me hate myself. _____

26. If I were to be myself all the time, I doubt I'd have any friends. _____

27. I think I'm on the same level with others. That helps me establish good relations with them. _____

28. People treat me differently than they treat others. _____

29. I live too much by other people's standards. _____

30. When I have to make a speech, I feel self-conscious and I know I'll be a terrible disappointment. _____

Scoring:

1. For items 2, 14, 21, 23, 27:

   If you answered 5, change your score to 1.

   If you answered 4, change your score to 2.

   If you answered 2, change your score to 4.

   If you answered 1, change your score to 5.

2. After these changes, add up your total score. The higher it is, the lower your self-love potential.

   Below 55: You are a self-loving person with a self-concept that's likely to help you. Congratulations!

   56–85: You are a good friend to yourself if not always the best. Work on it.

   86–115: You probably have loving feelings towards yourself about half of the time. Check out the following tips.

   115–140: You don't love yourself as much as you could. Look over the tips and get a self-esteem raising plan into action.

   Above 140: Time to get professional help and get back into a positive-feeling mode. Check out tips.

Four Love Yourself Better Tips

1. **Give yourself a doing-unto-others break.** Take yourself to lunch or dinner once a week. Take off your watch—and don't look at anybody else's; take your time. Do any fun nonroutine thing that enters your mind—walk or skip to the park, read your favorite childhood book, take a walk in the rain without your umbrella, swing on a swing, go down a slide, play on the monkey bars.

2. **Demonstrate your I'm-my-best-friend feelings** by taking out a gift of the month club membership for yourself. Get a treat, anything you love—cheeses, chocolates, CDs, novels, perfumes, massages—once a month.

3. **Make your body more lovable.** Spend money on a week at a spa or a health ranch. For double benefits, share the experience with a friend you'd like to know better.

4. **Read some books on self-improvement.** Check out the book list on the next page for a start, or look at the bibliography at the end of this book. Visit the library or a bookstore and browse the shelves.

Reading Material

You Can Heal Your Life, Louise Hay

The Miracle of Mindfulness, Thich Nhat Hanh

A Woman's Worth, Marianne Williamson

Succulent Wild Woman: Dancing With Your Wonder Full Self, Sark

The Healing of Emotion: Awakening the Fearless Self, Chris Griscom

There is Nothing Wrong With You: Regardless of What You Were Taught to Believe, Cheri Huber

Women of Courage: Inspiring Stories from the Women Who Lived Them, Katherine Martin

Fearless Creating: A Step-by-Step Guide to Starting and Completing Your Work of Art, Eric Maisel, Ph.D.

The Inner Child Workbook: What to Do With Your Past When It Just Won't Go Away, Cathryn Taylor

Embracing Your Inner Critic: Turning Self-Criticism Into a Creative Asset, Hal Stone, Ph.D. & Sidra Winkelman Stone, Ph.D.

One's Own Self, written and illustrated by Dori Jalazo (http://www.dorij.com)

Getting The Love You Want, Gerald Jampolsky

After evaluating how good of a friend you are to yourself, consider with whom you spend your time. As with the grains of sand, the more time we spend with someone the more likely we are to begin to look like them, and to pick up their characteristics. It is much like the old adage of "Choose your friends wisely and be careful who you associate with, you may become like them."

Often our relationships are based on a mutual interest, such as sports or hobbies or children. We may not have anything in common other than our mutual interest and after that interest fades, the friendship is gone. There is nothing wrong with this; in fact, it is a normal course of life—acquaintances come and go. The issue for us is to determine if these friends and acquaintances have a positive influence on our lives.

In fact, a good self-test for your current state of being is to take a long hard look at the personalities and energies of the people around you. Do they support you or put you down? Do you share the same value systems? Are they positive or negative? How do you feel when you're around them? Can you go to them if you have a problem? Or are you cautious around them because you are afraid if you let them know how you really feel or what you really think, they wouldn't want to be friends anymore?

Negative people can be draining, but even more so if we are co-erced into the position of always being the positive one to pull them out of their doldrums. This dynamic isn't healthy for either one of you. Many women have not learned how to take care of themselves, so their relationships are often based on trying to get someone else to do it. As babies, we learn to please our parents in order to get the desired love and attention. We want them to continue to take care of us. It is sur-vival. We are engaging and charming and persuasive in order to get what we want.

As writer Karen Turner explained in a *Yoga Journal* article called "Building the Sacred Vessel of Relationship," adult relationships con-tinue along the same lines. She writes that there is an unconscious tele-pathic agreement of give and take: "I'll be there for you and be who you want me to be if you will do the same for me."

She points out that this system doesn't work well. No matter how hard we try, other people are seldom able to fulfill our needs consis-tently or successfully, so we get disappointed and frustrated. We are then left with the reality that we either try to change the other people to better suit our needs (which never works), or we resign ourselves to accept less than we really want. Furthermore, when we're trying to give other people what they want, we almost invariably do things we don't really want to do and end up resenting them, either consciously or unconsciously.

If we are open and aware enough, we come to realize that it doesn't work to try to take care of ourselves by taking care of others. We understand that we're the only ones who can actually take good care of ourselves, so we might as well do it directly and allow others to do the same thing for themselves.

Additionally, Turner points out, "What does it mean to take care of yourself? For me, it means trusting and following my intuition. It means taking time to listen to all my feelings—including the feelings of the child within me that is sometimes hurt or scared—and responding with caring, love, and appropriate action. It means putting my inner needs first and trusting that as I do this, everyone else's needs will get taken care of and everything that needs to be done will get handled." [11]

Taking care of ourselves does not mean that we do it alone; otherwise, we could all live as hermits. We are social creatures and need the closeness of others around us. Taking care of ourselves means conducting our relationships, both with ourselves and others, with conscious integrity, being honest, and making sure that our intent is congruent with what we desire.

Learn Relaxation Techniques

Several relaxation techniques have already been mentioned in this book in earlier chapters. The important point is to find a technique that works for you and use it. Relaxation techniques can be as simple as being quiet for a few minutes and watching your breath. You can relax while driving the car (but not too much). I have even practiced relaxation techniques while running.

The important thing is to clear your mind of the current stress in the world around you. It is easiest to do this with the breath. People may take the act of breathing for granted, but many do not realize how important it is to breathe properly. The act of breathing supplies oxygen to the bloodstream, which is then transformed into energy that can be used by the organs and other body systems. Breathing is similar to the old-fashioned blacksmith's bellows (see figure 6.2). When the handles are lifted, the bellows are open and air comes in. When the handles are pressed down and the bellows are deflated, the air rushes out. The diaphragm works like bellows, expanding when you inhale and deflating when you exhale.

FIGURE 6.2

Breathing Is Like a Blacksmith's Bellows

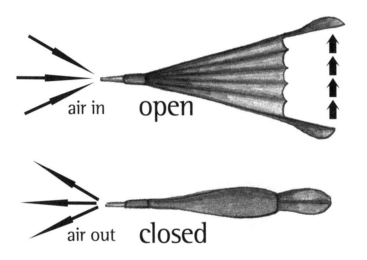

air in **open**

air out **closed**

This is the optimal form of breathing. Yet because of poor posture, health reasons, anxiety, stress, or habit, many of us do not breathe to our optimal capabilities. This means that we aren't getting the proper amount of oxygen to nourish our bodies and that we are weakening our systems.

What does a full breath feel like? While it isn't possible or necessary to fully expand the lungs on every breath, it helps for you to experience how it feels so that you can remind yourself to do this when you wish to relax or need a larger oxygen supply.

EXERCISE

Experiencing a Full Breath[12]

Try this exercise sitting, standing, and lying down.

1. Exhale deeply, contracting the belly.
2. Inhale slowly as you expand the abdomen.
3. Continue inhaling as you expand the chest.
4. Continue inhaling as you raise the shoulders up toward your ears.
5. Hold for a few comfortable seconds.
6. Exhale in reverse pattern, slowly. Release shoulders, relax chest, contract the belly.
7. Repeat.

This exercise will require gentle practice in order to reach the point where inhalation and exhalation are smooth and balanced. Beginners should only do this exercise two or three times continuously.

EXERCISE

Simple Breathing Exercises

When time is short, the following four exercises can be used quickly to refresh, help you focus, and relax.

1. Stand up. Bend from the waist; relax the knees and muscles around the perineum area. Place your hands on your upper thighs.

   Inhale deeply through the nose.

   Exhale forcefully through the mouth.

   Push all the air out of the lungs.

   Repeat.

2. Stand up. Raise arms above your head. Begin to jump up and down as if you were jumping rope.

   Inhale quickly as you jump up.

   When you land, expel air from your mouth with the sound of "hu."

   Continue for about thirty seconds.

   Stop. Allow your breath to come naturally.

3. Stand up. Inhale through the mouth as you raise your arms above your head. Pretend you are trying to grasp the stars. Get up on your tiptoes.

   Reach even higher, inhaling all the way.

   Release. Go limp.

   Exhale vigorously.

   Bend from the waist and let head and arms dangle like a rag doll.

   Stop.

   Breathe normally.[13]

4. Raise up on your tiptoes and stomp your heels down forcefully a few times. This serves to jar your body slightly and allows the tension to leave. I have found it to be effective during tennis matches and high anxiety times with family members.

A deeper relaxation is helpful when you have more time. The following is a progressive relaxation I used frequently when I taught yoga. It was amusing to the other members of the local Y who wondered what kind of class would put the participants to sleep.

EXERCISE

Progressive Relaxation

Lie down and get comfortable. Stretch your legs out. Let your arms and hands rest comfortably at your side. Begin to notice your breath. Imagine a bright ball of sunlight that starts at your toes. Tighten them, or curl them under as hard as you can for five seconds then let go. The ball of light helps to focus your attention on a specific part of your body and helps your muscles to feel warm and relaxed.

Now go from your toes up your legs, first your calves, then knees, and upper legs. Tighten your buttocks and loosen. Next your abdomen and the muscles around your rib cage. Tighten and release your chest (pectoral) muscles, and those in your shoulders.

Before moving up to the neck, make your hands into fists then relax. As you relax each area notice how you feel. Is there any lingering tightness? If so, you can tighten and relax again. Use the ball of sunlight to warm and help you melt the tension away.

Next tighten the neck muscles, then on to the muscles in

the face. Squeeze your muscles around your eyes, then relax. Scrunch your forehead and release. After you have progressively relaxed all the muscle groups, if you still feel tension, then tighten every muscle in your body all at once and release.

Give Up the Need to Be Right

Learn the art of "detachment" and give up the need to be right. In most situations, it is preferable to stay centered and detached from the chaos around you. Although passion and emotional intensity are useful tools to persuade and inspire people, they can also get in the way of normal day-to-day relationships.

We have all been around people who overdramatize small matters. In fact, we've probably done so ourselves. The emotional intensity, whether it is anger, fear, or self-righteous zeal, serves as a vacuum cleaner that "sucks out" our very sense of reason. It renders us weak to deal with the situation objectively, and we find ourselves in the vicious cycle of "reacting against" rather than acting towards the kind of communication we desire.

The art of "detachment" is easier for some people than others. I've watched my husband do this for years and thought he was distant or not interested in what was going on around him. I thought he had problems with conflict and avoided confrontations with the children rather than discipline them. I accused him of not being available to me and to our children. Although some of this may be true, the greater truth is that he has learned the art of detachment.

His manner of being matter of fact and acting *later* rather than sooner is a sign of wisdom and strength rather than weakness. He doesn't want conflict, and he avoids yelling and screaming. He simply chooses not to react, to instead be quiet and pick the right moment for discipline or imparting wisdom. He seldom gets into an escalation of power and always keeps his center.

How does he do this? Since my husband and I have different personalities and different aspects (he is a King and I am a Warrior), we have different ways of handling things. In other words, his method may not work for me. What is important is the result. I would say that he *can stay detached* from situations of intense emotional conflict because he just can. It isn't something he consciously thinks about doing. It's easier for him because he has made it a habit. He knows how because of lots and lots of practice.

As a woman Warrior how do I respond to emotionally intense situations? I react, of course. I put on my battle armor and join the fray. Hurl ultimatums. Coerce. Persuade and assert authority. And when all else fails, as a last resort, I crown myself the ultimate decision-maker: "What I say goes. End of discussion."

This might serve well in the army or with family members or children who are compliant and either very young or very mature, but it certainly doesn't serve well with a volatile personality such as my eldest son's. My attempts at disciplining him and allowing him to face the consequences for his actions have often resulted in escalation of power struggles ending badly for both of us. On days when I'm well rested and feeling strong, I hold my own. On others when I'm sick or didn't get enough sleep or am experiencing some inner conflicts of my own, I lose my center.

Over the years, I've tried everything. Prayer. Meditation. Running. Walking away. Taking care of my own needs first. Beating a pillow. Throwing a basketball in the garage. Behavior modification charts (for him not me). Contracts. Therapy. Reading. Talking with other people. More reading. Searching for someone else who could understand what I'm talking about. More reading. Asking my husband to step in and be more involved. More reading. Searching.

What I've discovered is that there is no magic pill. There is nothing that works all the time. If anything, I must constantly change to stay one step ahead of him. What worked yesterday will not work tomorrow. From the Self-Identification Test, I know that we are both Warriors. His chief stumbling block is that he is stubborn; mine is that I'm impatient. That sets us up for explosive confrontations. But I have discovered that if I stay *detached*, I am able to keep my center and be a more effective parent. I find that I don't have to apologize for yelling and losing my temper. He, in turn, is able to more clearly see his part in things without the mess of adding mine into the whole affair.

One Valentine's Day, the older two children begged me to stay in bed so they could prepare a surprise for me. A half hour later, they informed me that they had burnt half my breakfast, but that the other half was quite edible and served it to me in bed. It was sweet and such a heartfelt gesture I was overcome with love and hugged them both.

Not an hour later, I asked them both to help clean up the gigantic mess they had made in the kitchen, and the fireworks began. It deteriorated into both of them accusing the other of not helping. Finally, the oldest stated he simply wasn't going to do what I had asked. His words were challenging and insolent. I reminded him that we had a contract and part of that contract was obedience and respect for others, as well as doing chores when asked. The consequences were loss of privileges. He whined. He shouted. He wailed. I said nothing and was calm in my reserve not to get sucked into his rage. He saw that it was no use and started cleaning up the kitchen. In the end, I was proud, not because he finally did what I asked, but that we were able to work through the emotional intensity without me "losing my cool."

What did I do internally so that I didn't react to his provocations? I kept breathing and thought about "detachment." I saw my husband in my mind's eye and used him as a model of behavior. I let go of the need to control the situation, yet firmly stated what was going to happen. I stayed centered despite my son's efforts to pull me out of my center by any method possible.

He continued to complain and argue. This time I had to pull out the contract and warn him of the consequences. I won't say that I stayed perfectly detached and centered, but I did only veer off center by a few degrees. The result was that he lost privileges for that day, was given time-out outside for about thirty minutes, and had to do the work anyway. An hour later, he calmly came into my room and apologized for his behavior.

The point is that I didn't do anything fancy or elaborate. I merely applied something I knew at the appropriate time. Often it doesn't even matter what we do. If we do anything different at all, it changes the outcome and behavior of the other person. In my son's example, he didn't get the desired reaction and was forced to change his own behavior the first time. The second time when he didn't get what he wanted, he escalated his old behaviors to the extreme to provoke me. When he saw that even though I lost my temper, he wasn't going to get me to lose it to the point of yelling, he gave up. In the end, I felt good because I kept my center, showed him the boundary, and allowed him to feel the consequences of his own actions.

Whether you keep to your center by visualizing, breathing, praying, or reciting mantras or affirmations, it is important to try to do so for your well-being as well as for others around you. I often use humor to stay centered. I visualize all sorts of outlandish scenarios: a huge pair of scissors tied with a big pink bow, such those used at a ribbon-cutting ceremony, cutting the string attaching me to the person or situation; that I'm a ten-foot giant gorilla dressed up in a tutu trying to balance on a high wire; or that I'm a fierce Xena Warrior Princess pulling out my sword and every weapon conceivable in order to defend my center. If I know I'm going to face a difficult situation up-front, I visualize wearing a suit of armor, or my personal favorite, an astronaut space suit, so that nothing they say or do can harm me. I pray and ask God and every angel to help me. I surround myself with a cocoon of light to protect me from negative words and energy. Afterwards, I reflect and meditate on what went right and what went wrong. The point is to find something that works for you and have fun with it.

Books to Read

Emotional Alchemy: How the Mind Can Heal the Heart, Tara Bennett-Goleman

The Seven Acts of Courage, Robert E. Staub

Sacred Contracts, Carolyn Myss

Faith in the Valley, Iyanla VanZant

Thriving in 24/7: Six Strategies for Taming the New World of Work, Sally Helgesen

Have Faith in a Higher Power

All things are possible with God.

MATTHEW 19:26

Having faith in a higher power takes us out of our everyday existence and broadens our horizons to include others. It also expands our awareness and encourages us to be vulnerable. It also gives us support and helps us understand that we aren't doing this alone. Faith helps us to persevere and energizes us to create new possibilities. It helps us reach and go beyond our potential.

Caroline Myss writes in *Why People Don't Heal and How They Can*, "Our spiritual needs must be met if our bodies are to thrive. This realization has become a fundamental part of the processes of maintaining health and healing...Ultimately, everything we learn about our deeper selves enhances not only our health, but also the quality of our physical life."[14] The motto of the YMCA/YWCA is to be whole in body, mind, and spirit. If we are developed physically and mentally but not spiritually, we are still lacking and that internal homing mechanism will seek to fill the void.

The spiritual journey is a personal one. Having faith in a higher power is gratifying, assuring, and humbling. It teaches us about our place in the world, about living with other people, and of the miracle of life. Thousands of books have been written on having faith in a higher power. Seek people, places, and books to read or begin intuitively by praying and practicing silence. You may start by reading some of the books listed at the end of this section or by reviewing books listed in the bibliography.

Prayer of a Woman at Home

Explorer God,
You have put within us
A spirit of adventure
To move us beyond
The immediate
And to explore even
Our most familiar environment
To its fullest potential.
May each day become an
Adventure of people, tasks, places
And responsibilities.
And when I feel gray and lifeless
May your Spirit remind me that
Each day brings
Its own gifts
And that the best
Is yet to be.

KATHY KEAY
Laughter, Silence & Shouting:
An Anthology of Women's Prayers

Books to Read

Conversations With God, Neale Donald Walsch

Wisdom of the Ages: A Modern Master Brings Eternal Truth in Everyday Life, Wayne Dyer

The Miracle of Mindfulness, Thich Nhat Hanh

An Open Life: Joseph Campbell, John M. Maher and Dennie Briggs

Autobiography of a Yogi, Paramahansa Yogananda

One Day My Soul Just Opened Up: 40 Days and 40 Nights Towards Spiritual Strength and Personal Growths, Iyanla Vanzant

Wouldn't Take Nothing for My Journey Now, Maya Angelou

The Bible

Laughter, Silence & Shouting: An Anthology of Women's Prayers, Kathy Keay

Living in the Light, Shakti Gawain

The Michael Handbook, José Stevens and Simon Warwick-Smith

Handbook To Higher Consciousness, Ken Keyes

Illusions: The Adventures of a Reluctant Messiah, Richard Bach

Meditations & Inspirations, Virginia Satir

The Artist's Way, Julia Cameron

How To Know God: The Soul's Journey Into the Mystery of Mysteries, Deepak Chopra

God, Is That You?, Katharine Giovanni

Laugh, Play More and Have a Sense of Humor

The way to reconnect with our purpose is to do
things that seem at first appearance, to lack
purpose.

KENNETH MAUE

Many people are familiar with the following poem. After reading it, try
writing one of your own.

I'd Pick More Daisies

If I had my life to live over, I'd try to make more mistakes

Next time. I would relax. I would limber up. I would be sillier
than I have been this trip. I know of very few things I
would take seriously. I would be crazier. I would be less
hygienic. I would take more chances. I would take more
trips. I would climb more mountains, swim more rivers
and watch more sunsets...

I would eat more ice cream and less beans. I would have
more actual troubles and fewer imaginary ones. You see,
I am one of those people who lives prophylactically and
sanely and sensibly, hour after hour, day after day. Oh, I
have had my moments and if I had it to do over again, I'd
have more of them.

In fact, I'd try to have nothing else. Just moments, one after
another, instead of living so many years ahead each day.
I have been one of those people who never go anywhere
without a thermometer, a hot water bottle, a gargle, a
raincoat and a parachute. If I had it to do over again, I
would go places and do things and travel lighter than I
have.

If I had my life to live over, I would start barefooted earlier
in the spring and stay that way later in the fall. I would
play hooky more. I wouldn't make such good grades
except by accident. I would ride on more merry-go-
rounds. I'd pick more daisies.

NADINE STAIR, 87
Louisville, Kentucky

Humor and laughter are wonderful medicines. They can diffuse anger and remind us how temporary everything is. In her courageous book about surviving breast cancer, Laura Evans wrote that she was inspired by "I'd Pick More Daisies" to write one of her own. She began it, "When I am old..." and proceeded to write what she wanted to do since at that time she was given only six months to live.

She wrote, among many things, that she would get a tattoo when she was old, and she did. She didn't wait, because she didn't know if there would be a tomorrow. She continued to live the rest of her life making every moment count, not waiting until she grew old. Take the time to write your own "When I am old..." poem. What will yours say? Part of mine goes like this.

"When I Am Old..."

I will wear whatever makes me feel good. I will travel to parts unknown, blending in with the natives, soaking in their culture like a sponge. I will learn new languages. Taste new food. Listen to strange music. Dance new dances and sing new songs.

My home will feel peaceful, full of arts and books, poetry and plants, and music. I will kick-box and swing, run and climb mountains. I will snuggle with my husband in front of a fire in a snow-covered mountain lodge sipping amaretto and red wine.

I will teach and laugh and run in the rain. Sunbathe in the nude. Skinny dip in the Caribbean. Give my husband massages and get massages from him.

I will hug my grandchildren. Read them books. Teach them to love Emily Dickinson, Jane Austen, The Brontes, e e cummings and Whitman. I will pull back the furniture in our living room and dance with them until our sides ache.

Travel. Speak French. Write poetry. Buy trinkets and souvenirs. Wear sexy hose and outlandish hats.

Ignore important events. Celebrate silly ones.

Have a cottage garden. Eat chocolate. Shop with my daughter.

Play chess with my sons.

I will climb more mountains...perhaps more slowly and experience the joy of life...Rest.

> Have fun with life. Rent a comedy and watch the video with someone you love. Learn to laugh at yourself. Don't take life so seriously. There is no gold trophy at the end. Realize that what you create and do during your life on earth is up to you; what you think and what you do is what you get.

Develop a Personal Life Vision

Use your time and energy to realize your personal life vision. Developing a personal life vision is discussed in chapter 1.

> **Books to Read**
>
> *Visioneering*, Andy Stanley
>
> *Soul Catcher*, Kathy and Amy Eldon

Spend Time in Silence Every Day, Mediate and Pray

> I believe that God is in me as the sun is in the color and fragrance of a flower—the Light in my darkness, the voice in my silence.
>
> HELEN KELLER
> *Laughter, Silence, and Shouting:*
> *An Anthology of Women's Prayers*

Be still and know that I am God.

PSALMS 46:10

Silence allows us to move toward mindfulness. While spending time in the silence, practice paying attention to things. Pay attention to your body, to the small voice (intuition) inside that can give you answers to questions you never knew you had. You will find strength and solace in the silence.

> *The simplest questions*
> *Are the most profound.*
> *Where were you born? Where is your home?*
> *Where are you going? What are you doing?*
> *Think about these once in a while, and*
> *Watch your answers change.*

A friend of mine realized how much noise was in her life when she could only sit for twenty seconds in silence. Silence is the gift of tuning into ourselves.

There are many excellent ways for structuring your time so that you can get the most out of the silence. Sometimes it may help to start with something that inspires you: a song, a poem, an inspirational verse, a Bible passage, or other text that helps you to contemplate. Focus on what inspires you. Become single-minded; think only of that message and what it creates in you. Allow yourself to be fully immersed in its message. Don't control it; just let the feelings come.

Sometimes it is helpful to be still in the silence, and other times it is better to move. One technique that works for someone with a lot of energy is to practice "mindfulness" while walking.

EXERCISE

A Mindful Walk[15]

Find a quiet place where you can walk back and forth over about thirty feet. In each of the three parts of this exercise, simply note the sensations in your feet and legs as you lift and move each in turn. Whenever your mind wanders, bring it back to those sensations. Don't strain your neck by looking at your feet; keep a relaxed gaze at a point in front of you. Take twenty minutes for the entire exercise.

First Walk: Keep a normal pace, noting mentally "left" as you move your left foot forward and "right" as you move your right foot forward. Stay tuned to the sensations that go along with those movements.

Second Walk: Go a bit slower this time, and divide each step in your mind into "lifting" (leg goes up and forward) and "placing" (leg comes down). Finish one step completely before lifting the other foot.

Third Walk: Proceed at a much slower pace. Be aware of a three-part motion to each step: "lifting," "moving," then "placing." Try a snail's pace.

I have tried using these techniques in my backyard, at the beach, and in the mountains. You can also use them walking in the city (although it would be harder not to run into someone). The point is to single-mindedly focus on something so that you are not distracted by everything around you. This focus will help you go beyond what you perceive in your normal state of awareness. This is the same principle that has been used in ancient cultures, especially Asia, to heal, deepen spiritual insights, and provide a competitive edge in the martial arts. Recently there has been a lot of research on the effectiveness of meditation and spiritual practices in people suffering from chronic pain. This practice helps to reduce the suffering from the pain by separating the sensation from the emotional reaction to it.

Epiphany

What was invisible we behold,
What was unknown is known.
Open our eyes to the light of grace,
Unloose our hearts from fear,
Be with us in the strength of love,
Lead us in the hope of courage
Along the path of tribulation,
Till the overcoming is attained.

EVELYN FRANCES CAPEL
Laughter, Silence and Shouting:
An Anthology of Women's Prayers

It is important to spend time alone with God. We were put on earth to fulfill certain purposes, some individual and some that involve a larger community than ourselves. My theory is that God equipped us with a homing device that I envision as a large oval light pulsing in our bodies near our heart. God guides us using this beacon to the most desirable path for our life. When we are going along that path, things feel right. Even if trouble comes our way, we know we're doing the right thing. We don't have to ask anybody. We don't need therapy or even a good friend to tell us; we know that we're on our way. The more time we spend alone with God the easier this is to accomplish.

The trouble comes when we veer off the path. Because of free will and a stubborn human nature, we get curious and go off on side paths because they're tempting and because we crave adventure. It isn't too long before we feel something. Perhaps a nagging thought. Or our bodies are tired from too much indulgence. If we've spent time in silence enough to listen to that small voice, we know enough to honor it and go back to the main path. If we haven't, then we often continue down the side path until the homing device becomes more insistent. "Turn back. Rocks ahead!" it screams. If we're open to it, we pay attention and turn around. If not, it may take an accident, a divorce, or the death of a loved one to force us to focus and listen to that small voice. It forces us to go into the silence.

How much easier it would be to give ourselves the time to do it willingly instead of being forced and directed by problems. There is a great deal of power in prayer and the time we spend in meditation. It not only helps us to listen to our inner voices and spend time with God; it also gives us a much-needed break from the excesses and stress of the world. And a side benefit is that it helps to conserve our energy, thereby keeping us younger. It is the closest thing we can come to the "fountain of youth."

> You are led through your lifetime
> By the inner learning creature,
> The playful spiritual being
> That is your real self.
>
> Don't turn away from possible futures
> Before you're certain you don't have
> anything to learn from them.
> You're always free
> To change your mind and
> Choose a different future,
> Or a different past.
>
> UNKNOWN

Give Time and Energy to Others, Volunteer

"I am stressed! There is always too much to do. I can't get it all done."

"I am overworked and overwhelmed with responsibility. My husband is always working. I feel angry. My family lives all over the country. I don't have any support systems. I have no social life or outlets. How can I make this better? How do I take care of myself so that I don't fall victim to heart attack or disease?"

Answer: "Become involved in your community by volunteering."

ANSWERED BY REDFORD WILLIAMS, M.D., AT A LECTURE
IN EDMONTON, CANADA, OCTOBER 28, 1994.

It is a wonderful paradox, but the more you give the more you receive. All my life, people have marveled at how much energy I have. I seem to be able to do a lot of things and when people ask me how I manage, I tell them I just do what I've always done. I find that the more I give, the more I get back. The more I do, the more I find the time and energy to accomplish. It is as if I gain momentum and the giving builds on itself. Although there is a point of diminishing returns, it all comes back to intent.

When I am giving (or volunteering) because I feel I have to or because I want to gain favor in some way, it tires and wears on me. When I feel led to give, I gain energy and happily accomplish great things.

Keeping to yourself may be necessary at times, but if you feel led to give and serve, you may find you actually gain more in the giving. An older acquaintance of mine kept to herself and didn't want to be bothered by other people. She loved her yard and craft projects, but had no time for neighborhood children or activities. Because of a family emergency, she was asked to give blood. While at the hospital, she saw an older woman holding infants in the nursery. The woman was part of a volunteer program. After learning more about the program, my unsociable acquaintance began volunteering, too. Being with the infants became the highlight of her week. At first reluctant to give to others, she opened up and gained much more.

Ask yourself: Where can I serve? What am I doing when I have the deepest satisfaction in giving to others? Reinforce these feelings and direct your efforts to make a positive impact. Give from your heart rather than from a feeling of obligation.

> Half the world is on the wrong scent in the pursuit of happiness. They think it consists in having and getting, and in being served by others. Rather, it consists in giving and in serving others.
>
> HENRY DRUMMOND

Rekindle a Sense of Place and Reconnect With Nature

> Fix all this in your memory. This spot is yours. This morning you saw, and that was the omen. You found this spot by seeing. The omen was unexpected, but it happened. You are going to hunt power whether you like it or not. It is not a human decision, not yours or mine. Now, properly speaking, this hilltop is your place, your beloved place; all that is around you is under your care. You must look after everything here and everything will in turn look after you.
>
> CARLOS CASTANEDA
> *The Journey to Ixtlan (Simon and Schuster, 1972)*

Throughout the past century, we have tried to distance ourselves from nature. We put it into parks and zoos. We developed the scientific model until it became our natural law so that we could fit life itself into rigid categories: medicine, law, education, and business. We have lost sight of the fact that we are nature and need to find our way back to a sense of unity with it.

Many of us have lost our sense of connectedness to the land. Because of our fast-paced lifestyles, we don't take the time to slow down and experience the outside—nature, the world around us. We underestimate the effect that place has on our character and destiny.

France's President Francois Mitterand said in the French magazine *L'Autre Journal* that "the American spirit is fired by the journey, the adventure, the departure by this need to escape, to go wherever your steps lead, to get away. From what? From convention, from home. Maybe—who knows?—from oneself, from death. One is looking for a better world and that inevitably lies beyond the horizon."[16]

In the Western world, we teach our children to dissect and analyze. The result is a world with children who are out of touch with living things. In her book, *The Second Self: Computers and the Human Spirit,* Sherry Turkle talks about how the computer is the main carrier of our psychological yardstick. Once upon a time we measured our talents and abilities by nature and we associated our moods and feelings with changes in the land or in the seasons. Now, Turkle believes, we look for our reflection in machines.

She illustrates her theory with this story of a fourth grade boy she found in the corner of a schoolyard, killing ants.

"Why are you doing that?" she asked.

"They're not alive," the boy explained. "So it's okay to crush them."

"But how do you know?"

"Because they do not think."

This dialogue is telling because it illustrates an unconscious, but widespread belief that reason is the only thing of value.

Valerie Andrews writes in her article, "Rekindling a Sense of Place," from the magazine *Common Boundary,* "To counter these trends, we must create new initiation rites that will help us establish a feelings connection to the natural world. Our young people need to have an intense and sobering experience, in which they earn the right to be on this earth. If they are not given this opportunity to stand up to nature, they will learn a form of abdication and begin to turn their backs on life."[17]

If we wish to rekindle a sense of place, our childhood memories are a good place to start. Think of a place where you felt safe as a child. For me, it was a large lake at the end of my street. When I was upset with my parents or just wanted to think, I would ride my bike or walk to the lake and sit for a long time just staring at the water. Sometimes I would feed the ducks. Sometimes I would take a book to read, and other times I would write.

I loved that place. It held a great deal of power for me. Even now, if I want to simulate that experience, I often seek other lakes, where I can sit in silence, feeling that same sense of connectedness, that same peacefulness that I remembered as a child.

Some people gravitate to the ocean, others to the mountains. Some like to go to dramatic places, such as Macchu Picchu, the majestic Rockies, the big surfs of Hawaii, or the Grand Canyon. Every place has its own energy. Some places, because of their geological and geographical makeup, actually are places of power. There are numerous materials written about magnetic and electrical energy fields occurring naturally in certain places on earth. Frances Nixon of British Columbia proposed the thesis in *Mysteries of Memory Unfold* that "all healthy people have a built-in navigational system, which orients them to the earth's magnetic fields."[18] She reports that, with a little practice, most people can sense the direction of their place of birth, as well as the directions of the compass, unless they have suffered head injuries, electrical shocks, or brain damage due to certain chemicals. Using a variety of physical exercises, which "cleanse" a person's field, Nixon and a number of doctors who have learned her Vivaxis system report that when people recover their ability to sense their direction of birth, they almost always become healthier.

Carl Jung said, "As scientific understanding has grown, so our world has become dehumanized. Man feels himself isolated in the cosmos, because he is no longer involved in nature and has lost his emotional 'unconscious identity' with natural phenomenon…Thunder is no longer the voice of an angry god, nor is lightning the avenging missile. No river contains a spirit, no tree is the principle of life in man, no snake contains the embodiment of wisdom, no mountain cave is the home of a demon. No voices now speak to man from stones, plants, or animals;

nor does he speak to them believing they can hear. His contact with nature has gone, and with it has gone the profound emotional energy that this symbolic connection supplied."[19]

To reconnect with nature, we need to learn how to talk to it and listen. Although sacred or power places seem to have some of the strongest voices, it is possible to connect right where you are. Find a place where you feel comfortable, a place that brings you happiness, and start there.

Develop a Sense of Community

It is something we yearn for. In my neighborhood, we seldom see our neighbors. Most of the time, we pass each other in our cars hurrying off to work, appointments, or children's activities. We stay cool inside our air-conditioned homes and come out only to cut the grass or take out the garbage. Occasionally, we'll wave at each other, but for the most part we don't connect unless there is some sort of disaster. We have a vague awareness that we feel isolated, but are too busy with our to-do lists to examine our separateness. Most of us are just plain exhausted. We've become self-contained.

What we often fail to recognize is that all of us depend on something outside of ourselves for survival. We aren't really separate. Fritjof Capra writes in *The Turning Point* that we live in a globally interconnected world in which the social, environmental, and psychological aspects are interdependent. The way we live our lives affects not only the people around us, but the greater community as well. For example, if the town in which we live has a shortage of water or living space or food, we must rely on people outside our immediate environment. If we pollute the air from car exhaust and cause holes in the ozone layer, it affects people around the globe. If we buy garments or running shoes made in Indonesia, it supports people half a continent away. So instead of being alone we are very much a part of a greater community. There is no "them," because the "them" is us.

When we cut ourselves off from each other and create separateness, the "wholeness" is split. We find it more difficult to experience joy and fulfillment. We find it occasionally through a movie, a TV show, a sexual relationship, a sumptuous dinner, a purchase of a long-awaited piece of art, but we find the joy temporary and fulfillment fleeting.

I find it more satisfying in the clamor of family get-togethers—sitting around the dinner table, dirty dishes and glasses strewn about, rehashing old stories and singing songs while my husband plays his guitar. Because his mother and father came from West Virginia, they'd always request John Denver's "Country Roads" and nobody cared whether we were off-key or even knew all the words. When we came to the chorus:

> "Country roads, take me home, to the place I belong, West
> Virginia, Mountain Mama, take me home, country roads."

Everyone sang as loudly as they could. We all felt connected. Somehow through the music and the good times, we bonded to feel like family, like we belonged together, as if we were a community.

Unfortunate as it may seem, we also feel connected during tragedy. During September of 1989, Hurricane Hugo struck the city we lived in at the time, Charlotte, North Carolina. It was unheard of that a hurricane with winds gusting over one hundred miles per hour would hit so far inland, and it caused considerable damage. We were without power for two weeks, and the city looked as if it had been bombed. Trees were down everywhere, roads were impassable, and stores were closed. No one could drive because the roads were blocked, and no one could buy gas even if they could get their cars out.

My brother says he loves natural disasters. An environmentalist and cynic, he says, "There's nothing like a good natural disaster to bring people together. People come out of their homes to chain-saw trees, help their neighbors dig out from under debris, shovel out from under the snow, and share food and stories." For that moment, we bond. We feel the intimacy. We feel a part of something bigger than ourselves.

The sad part comes when we go back to living the way we did before the disaster. We seem to forget the belonging, the closeness, the sharing. We go back to waving from car windows and back to our air conditioning. It seems that there can be so much more.

Our neighborhood was amazing. Most of us knew each other but had little time to visit because we worked or were busy with our children and their activities. After Hugo, we prepared most of our meals together so we could use up the food in our freezers before it went bad. One neighbor, an ex-Marine, organized a "chain-saw brigade" and cleared trees from the road. Other neighbors checked in on homes like ours, which were among the worst hit. There was such a great outpouring of love and support. We all felt nurtured, and we all felt the connection. We wanted the intimacy to continue, but it wasn't to be. Sadly after the lights came back on, we all retreated back into our homes—to our own freezers, televisions, carpools and busy schedules—and we lost the connection. A few of us dared bring up the subject, but none of us knew how to change it. "That's just the way it is" was the frequent reply. "What else can we do?" was often heard.

Good question. What else can we do? Well, the first step is recognizing the need for feeling connected, the way it feels when you're not connected, and the way it feels when you are. Then nurture that connection.

Since 1974, the General Social Survey has chronicled the habits of Americans. Response to "How often do you spend a social evening with a neighbor?" shows attendance even once a year at such an event has declined from 72 percent in 1974 to 61 percent in 1993. The number of Americans who report that they have attended a public meeting on town or school affairs has fallen—from 22 percent in 1973 to 13 percent in 1993. Similar declines have occurred for attendance at political rallies or speeches and for serving on committees of local organizations. Church attendance has declined at least 20 percent since the 1960s.[20]

My husband recently commented that next year he wanted to do something different to really feel connected at Christmas. He said he didn't feel it this Christmas, and he missed that feeling. We talked about ways to do that. Perhaps sponsor a family and have them come to our house for Christmas Eve or Christmas Day. Even though we financially sponsored a family for Christmas, just giving the money didn't give the feeling of intimacy or connectedness to others. We discussed having each family member select a person to do kind things for each month throughout the year. And while good ideas, I know in my heart that they will fail, unless we go into the space of silence and become more balanced ourselves before looking to others to fill the void.

While noble, even the act of doing something for someone else in order to feel connected or peace or fulfilled is still off the mark. It starts inside first, then the other things follow. It's the next step up on the soul's evolutionary trail. *The Bible* states in I Corinthians 3 that the temple of God is within ourselves. So the key is finding the balance and centering within ourselves.

There are many things that can be done, and some ideas are offered at the end of this section. By getting involved, through volunteer work or even being more intimate with your neighbors and friends, you will be promoting a sense of community. The important point is to eliminate the us versus them mentality and to realize that we are all in this together.

Another way of looking at being part of a community is to support family and friends, especially in their time of need. A friend shared a story about how she and her suite-mates from college at the University of North Carolina-Chapel Hill came together years later to help one of the group cope with breast cancer. One of the roommates had to undergo a double radical mastectomy as well as extensive chemotherapy. The college friends banded together and pooled their divergent talents and resources together to help their friend through her hard time. One helped her husband find a job, after he lost his because of needing to care of his convalescing wife. Another provided a home for them to live in and clothing for the family when they lost everything they owned due to financial burdens. All of them came together to support their friend emotionally when she was too depressed to go on. Even though they gave their time and money, what they gained was so much more. They reveled in being needed and being able to help an extraordinary woman in an extraordinary way.

Another example is a tennis friend who was severely injured when she tried to stop her car from rolling backwards down a hilly driveway and into a group of children playing in the street. She was getting out of the car when it started rolling. Without thinking about the consequences to her, she tried to stop the car and, in the process, was dragged and almost pinned under the car. The upper layer of the skin on her leg and arm was scraped totally off her body. Her middle and lower skin layers were exposed, bloody, and raw. Although she had stopped the car enough to ensure the safety of the children, she was critically hurt.

My friend is an avid tennis player and is well-known in the community. Later in sharing her story, she said that she was most impressed by the overwhelming outpouring of love and support from her tennis friends. She received countless cards, visitors, and well-wishers during her hospital stay and months of rehabilitation. She said her tennis "family" offered more care and attention than her extended family, which lived too far away.

She was amazed that so many people cared about her enough to call, write, and stop by. Normally, this woman was the one giving to others. She routinely sent friends and tennis acquaintances birthday cards or notes to cheer them. She said the experience of receiving was so new to her, she hardly knew how to react. The love she felt was so overwhelming, it was hard for her to accept, but it also felt so good that she wanted to share the love she felt with others.

Recommendations for Building Community

1. **Begin where you are.** Do you have friends, family, or coworkers around you that would benefit from your support or the support of each other? If so, encourage the members of this informal community to interact positively with each other.

2. **Look at your relationships with others.** Are you the one who normally calls and reaches out to your friends, or do they call you? If you are the one calling, start asking for people in your life to help you when you need help. If you are the one who is normally on the receiving end, start "passing it forward" and giving some of what you are receiving to others in need.

3. **Develop informal or formal support groups.** What are your interests? Books? Join or start a book club. Writing? Try doing the same. Get like-minded individuals together and have informal discussions periodically.

4. **Read a book about developing community.** The following are some suggested places to begin.

Building Communities from the Inside Out: A Path Toward Finding and Mobilizing a Community's Assets, John P. Kretzmann and John L. McKnight

Community Building on the Web: Secret Strategies for Successful Online Communities, Amy Jo Kim

Building a Writing Community: A Practical Guide, Marcia Freeman

Building Communities of Learners: A Collaboration Among Teachers, Students, Families and Community, Sudia Paloma McCaleb

Community Building: Renewal, Well-Being, and Shared Responsibility, Patricia L. Ewalt, editor

A Place To Remember: Using History To Build Community, Robert R. Archibald

The Diversity Advantage, Lenora Billings-Harris

Teach and Mentor What You Know and Are Learning

Certain cultures through history have understood and honored the wisdom of their elders and ancestors. Instead of looking towards the newest and latest invention, they used lessons passed down from family to family to help them plan for future generations. In American culture, we learn how this worked from our Native American heritage, but often find ourselves living for today, using more than we give back, and not planning for future generations.

The folly of this path is clearly demonstrated in the following adaption of the famous words of Chief Seattle:

How can you buy the sky?
How can you own the rain and the wind?

My mother told me,
Every part of this earth is sacred to our people.
Every pine needle. Every sandy shore.
Every mist in the dark woods.
Every meadow and humming insect.
All are holy in the memory of our people.

My father said to me,
I know the sap that courses through the trees
As I know the blood that flows in my veins.
We are part of the earth and it is part of us.
The perfumed flowers are our sisters.

The bear, the deer, the great eagle, these are our brothers.
The rocky crests, the meadows,
The ponies—all belong to the same family.
The voice of my ancestors said to me,
The shining water that moves in the streams and rivers is
Not simply water, but the blood of your grandfather's
    grandfather.
Each ghostly reflection in the clear waters of the lakes tells
Of memories in the life of our people.

The water's murmur is the voice of your great-great-
    grandmother.
The rivers are our brothers. They quench our thirst.
They carry our canoes and feed our children.
You must give to the rivers the kindness you would give
To any brother.

The voice of my grandfather said to me,
The air is precious. It shares its spirit with all
The life it supports. The wind that gave me my first
Breath also received my last sigh.
You must keep the land and air apart and sacred,
As a place where one can go to taste the wind that
Is sweetened by the meadow flowers.

When the last Red Man and Woman have vanished with
   their wilderness,
And their memory is only the shadow of a cloud moving
   across
The prairie, will the shores and forest still be here?
Will there be any of the spirit of my people left?
My ancestors said to me, This we know:
The earth does not belong to us. We belong to the earth.

The voice of my grandmother said to me,
Teach your children what you have been taught.
The earth is our mother.
What befalls the earth befalls all the sons and daughters
Of the earth.

Hear my voice and the voice of my ancestors,
The destiny of your people is a mystery to us.
What will happen when the buffalo are all slaughtered?
The wild horses tamed?
What will happen when the secret corners of the forest are
   heavy with the scent of many men?

When the view of the ripe hills is blotted by talking wires?
Where will the thicket be? Gone.
Where will the eagle be? Gone!
And what will happen when we say good-bye to the swift
   pony and the hunt?
It will be the end of living, and the beginning of survival.

This we know:
All things are connected like the blood that unites us.
We did not weave the web of life,
We are merely a strand in it.
Whatever we do to the web, we do to ourselves.

We love this earth as a newborn loves its mother's heartbeat.
If we sell you our land, care for it as we have cared for it.
Hold in your mind the memory of the land as it is when you
   receive it.
Preserve the land and the air and the rivers for your
Children's children and love it as we have loved it.

*Excerpted from Chief Seattle's speech in 1854 in response to the
U.S. Government pushing for an exhausted and beleaguered
Native American nation to sell its land.*

Teaching and mentoring is an essential part of the process of ensuring that information is passed on. It is so much easier and more efficient for the human race to not have to keep reinventing the wheel. If you know something, pass it on. If you really want to learn something, teach it.

There is an old adage that says, "Teach what you need to learn" and it normally holds true. There is one type of understanding that comes with reading or listening; it involves staying in the mind. Yet applying this knowledge involves a different set of skills. Have you ever tried to get up in front of a group of people and make a presentation on material you thought you knew and when you tried to explain it, found yourself tongue-tied? "It's like, well, you know..." Teaching something, whether a skill or a concept, means you have to integrate it into your awareness so much that you are able to explain this knowledge in enough different ways to ensure that the student is able to understand what you are trying to get across. In other words, you have to know the material or information well enough to be able to give it to the receiver in a way that he or she will be able to take in, which may be different from the way you learned it.

For example, if I want to teach a woman about getting in touch with her intuitive side, I would start by finding out more about her. How does she like to get information: visually, by listening to it, or by having some sort of physical experience? If she is a visual learner, I might start by encouraging the student to read a book first, then talk about what she learned. If she is more of an auditory learner, I might explain some ideas to her first, have a discussion, then ask the student to explore more information on the topic so that we can discuss it the next time. If the student is more of a kinesthetic learner, I would encourage her to start with a meditation exercise, then journal her experience. I may choose to do all three with any type of learner, but it would be most important for me to be open to the student's experience of the education process. How is the student responding? What excites her? What motivates her to learn?

A good coach or teacher knows how to do this. In fact, they do it instinctively. Recently, Oprah Winfrey wrote about her relationship with Maya Angelou in *O Magazine*. She explained that she resonated with Angelou because of similar life experiences. Winfrey looks up to Angelou as a kind of "quintessential Everywoman: essayist, entertainer, activist, poet, professor, film director, and mother" who recently conducted the Boston Pops simply because she felt like doing it. More importantly, though, Winfrey likes the respect, care, and attention Angelou gives to their relationship. Winfrey explained about a time when Angelou was overseas and Winfrey needed to talk to her. When Winfrey was told that Angelou was onstage in the middle of a speech, Winfrey said that she needed to talk with Angelou immediately. When Angelou got to the phone, she didn't answer with a "You just interrupted me"; she sent a "What is it, baby?" full of genuine love, caring, and devotion across the transatlantic lines.

Winfrey notes that she has gained wisdom and insight from Angelou, who taught her that "modesty speaks volumes about falseness" and that as soon as that "modest" person is slammed by the harsh reality of life, his or her modesty soon falls away. Angelou says that it is much better to be truthful, to be who you really are.

Angelou also has taught Winfrey about setting high standards. Angelou doesn't tolerate negativity in her house and will not stay in a place that feels negative to her. She doesn't tolerate racial slurs and believes that we can't allow ourselves to be "pecked to death by ducks," which is her way of describing people "who reduce your humanity through what Jules Feiffer called little murders." They don't have enough courage to go ahead and bushwhack you to your face. Instead, they might do or say something negative, and then say, "Oh, I didn't really mean it," or they are covert about what they do. The effect is still to demean us, certainly not to make us stronger.

This phenomenon of covertness is all too often prevalent in the way women treat each other. As previously mentioned, girls learn to be "covert" rather than "overt" in dealing with their feelings. These same little girls then grow into adult women who smile and say to your face, "Of course, I think you're doing a marvelous job!" then turn to a coworker and whisper, "I can't believe she's going ahead with that project. I wouldn't be caught dead doing it that way!"

The problem with covert behavior is that is gets in the way of the teaching and mentoring process. A good mentor is by definition someone higher up in an organization or with more wisdom in a certain area that can take a promising younger or less experienced initiate under her wing. This relationship would be closer than the average manager-subordinate, or teacher-student relationship and would involve:

➤ Being a guide through the intricacies of the unwritten rules of the organizational culture.

➤ Being a safe haven for "venting" or sounding off about feelings and ideas.

➤ Serving as a base to encourage the protégé to see the reality of a given situation.

➤ Providing individual development information, such as further education ideas; teaching the politics of a given organization or situation; and giving the protégé access to the "right people."

➤ Being a champion or PR person for the protégé when appropriate opportunities come along.

➤ Establishing the image to the prevailing culture that the protégé is valued by the mentor; thereby providing the protégé with the image of power and upward mobility.

Even though Maya Angelou and Oprah Winfrey are not working together in the same organization, their relationship can be seen as a mentor-protégé using the aforementioned criteria. Many women have wished they had someone to show them the way, someone to help them answer the questions: What decisions should I make? What are the ramifications of my decision? What are my alternatives? Am I thinking clearly? Am I seeing current reality?

Countless times I've wished for a mentor myself. I've prayed for someone to come into my life to teach me and point out the roadblocks in order to accelerate my learning. Sometimes I've been lucky enough to have a mentor, but they don't stay long. My mentors are situational. They come and go when the need arises, and then either they or the need for them passes on.

I believe that the value of being mentored is that it speeds up the learning process. A mentor is someone who can point out the reality of the situation and can guide you through the process of dealing with it. A really good mentor won't do it for you, or may not even give you the answers, but she will ask questions to encourage you to come up with the answers yourself. A really good mentor will be supportive of you throughout this process and will help you play back the significance of an event in order find its essential message. They teach you the language that helps you listen to your own heart. They celebrate your mistakes as well as your triumphs and, in doing so, encourage your transformation.

Just imagine how wonderful it would be to have more people be conscious mentors; to have more people consciously helping others along their path; to encourage their own search; to create an environment of empowerment within ourselves and within each other.

Live Your Life With Integrity and From the Heart

In the end, all we have left is who we are and how we live our lives. Integrity means that we are living our lives in alignment with our true purpose or values. Living from the heart means that we connect to others with the clearest intent, that the window of our relationships is as free from distortion and is as close to being real as we can possibly make it. When we are connecting to people from the heart, they can feel it. They respond in kind, and together we start on the spiral of our greatest potential. When we withhold and come into relationships with distortions of fear and anger, people respond in kind and we begin the downward spiral into negativity and lose our potentiality.

Each night after I give my children their goodnight kisses, I pull an imaginary thread through my heart and from across the room pull it through their's, while we both say together: "From my heart to yours and your heart to mine." I started doing this one time when my daughter was away from home and homesick. It was a way that she could anchor my love into her being and feel me close to her even when I wasn't physically there. It worked and became a nightly ritual.

Although those words may not be appropriate with everyone we meet, it can make a difference when we reach out to others to form connections. To the people we reach out to, we say: "I see through to the real part of you, to who you really are. It is okay, however you want to be. Now just breathe."

Heart Healing

We are together—
Joined by a shimmering
strand of humanity.
Yet suffer the illusion of separation,
Compounded by heavy-lidded eyes
Glassy with forgetfulness and
cloudy with the drink of carnality.

Only heart,
that pulsing, throbbing emblem of life
Can strip the veil
and unleash the power of
Truth, and Love:
The explosion of knowledge that
is the remembering,
of what we have already forgotten.

DEBRA J. GAWRYCH
January 19, 2001

CHAPTER SEVEN

THE HEROINE'S JOURNEY: PART II

Then We Learn To Live With Each Other

To see a world in a grain of sand
And a heaven in a wildflower:
Hold infinity in the palm of your hand,
And eternity in an hour.

WILLIAM BLAKE

When you are inspired by some great
Purpose, some extraordinary project,
All your thoughts break their bonds;
Your mind transcends limitation,
Your consciousness expands in every direction,
And you find yourself in a new, great
And wonderful world.
Dormant forces, faculties and talents
Become alive, and you discover yourself
To be a greater person by far
Than you ever dreamed
Yourself to be.

PATANJALI
First to Third Century B.C.

IT ALL COMES DOWN TO THIS. Alone you can accomplish fantastic, wonderful things, but together, with other women, the sisterhood, we can accomplish: the unbelievable, the remarkable, the everlasting. As you work on yourself and come together with other women, consider looking through the sisterhood. On the other side of the glass are all the possibilities brought about by inspiration. They are limitless. There are some we've already thought of and more we have not. The heroine's journey includes going inside to discover insight so you are stronger and then coming back into the world to use that insight.

The knowledge gained from self-discovery can be used to support other women. Eventually, we will make the discovery that our differences and likenesses can together be used to solve greater problems than our own. It is about inspiration—inspiring each other to become bigger and better than what we were before.

There is nothing noble in being superior to
someone else. The true nobility is in being
superior to your previous self.

CELEBRATING WOMEN

Together we can learn from our failings. We can help each other. Our intentions may sometimes fall short of what we desire, but we'll be there to help pull each other through. We may forget our place and trample on someone else, and the sisterhood is there to encourage us to be forgiving, both to ourselves and to the other person, so that out of guilt we don't perpetuate the cycle.

The possibilities are limitless. Looking through the glass, we can see women supporting each other in small groups across the country. Through common interests they are gathering: to pray or read, to minister to the sick, to tend to the elderly, to garden in the city. Perhaps it is a group of policewomen or women in the military who need to feel the support, share the experiences, and seek the advice of other women in what has traditionally been a male role. Perhaps it is a group of homemakers who need to feel connected to other women in some way other than only through their children. The common thread is that they are being supportive of one another, strangers and friends alike, bonding through a common purpose.

Together we can resurrect the spirit of community. We can watch our intent with our fellow neighbors and become involved. We can begin by nurturing the spirit of community among our friends and acquaintances, even our colleagues at work. Instead of pie-in-the-sky mumbo jumbo, we can live the life we were taught very young: "Treat other people as you would have them treat you."

Women in the sisterhood today have an unprecedented amount of freedom. We are freer than men to explore a full range of emotions just because we're women and are "supposed" to have such feelings. If we choose, we can be a breadwinner or homemaker. Thanks to the pioneering work of many women over the past two centuries, women have achieved equal status through legislation and through changes in social attitudes.

Although some may complain that women are treated unfairly and are not given their due, I would offer to you to consider that there are no victims. Any group or segment of the population can feel victimized if they look closely enough. It is an issue of not dividing the world into "us" versus "them." It is an issue of shifting perspective, of seeing the world as, "together we can accomplish great things."

There was a popular song in the early '70s with the lyrics: "United we stand, divided we fall..." and it holds as true today as then. It doesn't serve a purpose for women to put each other down by saying, "So who does she think she is" when one of the sisterhood achieves success. There is no need for a survival-of-the-fittest attitude among women, for women to fight and claw to "get or keep their man" or to land the best job. There is no need to put another woman down because we feel threatened. Another woman's success does not mean we should think any less of ourselves. Instead, it means that we rejoice in her success because it is really our own. She is us. She has achieved her success because of who we are. And we have achieved ours because of her.

When we really get that we are not "apart" from each other, but all together "a part" of something larger, then we will be able to honor all of the sisterhood. And then that glass window that is the sisterhood will be clean and free of distortions and cracks. It will let the truth of our existence shine through.

The sisterhood teaches us about integrating the various aspects of our nature into a harmonious existence with other women. Yet as illustrated throughout this book, the ability to be in harmonious relationship with others is limited or mirrored by the degree to which we have achieved that harmony or integration within ourselves. Integrating what we have learned helps us come to a point of wholeness, a point of wellness. This does not occur in the abstract, but through experience.

Integration takes place not only with intellectual understanding, but also in the physical, emotional, and spiritual part of our nature. True integration is experienced as an "Aha!" that occurs at such a powerful frequency level it permeates the cellular structure of our bodies. It delves into the deepest emotional states and vibrates into our less conscious and more intangible being. Furthermore, the impact of this experience can also transcend an individual and can affect others around her. It is much like what happens when a rock is thrown into a lake. The rock smashes through the smooth surface and plunges into the depths. At the surface, ever-expanding concentric circles begin at the point of impact and slowly make their way out until they disappear. The effect of this impact has far-reaching implications for changing the surface of the lake as well as for changing the dynamics of relationship when the impact occurs in our daily lives.

The more integrated we become, the more "whole" we are and the more we enter into our relationships from that perspective. This state of "wholeness," or the search for achieving it, is a wonderful way to begin consciously taking our place in the sisterhood.

> *"Next time I see you, I'll take your hand, look you in the eye, and say hello! What can I do for you, dear friend? How has your journey been? Come let us see to this adventure together."*

Debra J. Gawrych

Praise to the Women on My Journey

To the women on my journey

Who showed me the ways to go and ways not to go,

Whose strength and compassion held up a torch of light
And beckoned me to follow,

Whose weakness and ignorance darkened the path and
Encouraged me to turn another way.

To the women on my journey

Who showed me how to live and how not to live,

Whose grace, success and gratitude lifted me into the
fullness of surrender to God,

Whose bitterness, envy and wasted gifts warned me away
from the emptiness of self-will.

To the women on my journey

Who showed me what I am and what I am not,

Whose love, encouragement and confidence held me
Tenderly and nudged me gently,

Whose judgment, disappointment and lack of faith called
Me to deeper levels of commitment and resolve.

To the women on my journey who taught me love by
Means of both darkness and light,

To these women I say *bless you* and *thank you* from the
depths of my heart, for I have been healed and set free
through your joy and through your sacrifice.

REV. MELISSA M. BOWERS
Chicken Soup for the Woman's Soul

By a Friend

Say to me what you really mean
I won't ever give you reason to lie
See into me, what I am is in my eyes
And I'm willing to believe the same in you

I think I'm ready now, I'm only learning how
Is there anyone around who has a plan?
I'm not a lonely man, there are those who think I am
But I'd rather be alone until I'm standing by a friend

By a friend I've known only minutes
By a friend I've known all my life
To you friend I say let us go outside and play
In the laughter, in the rain
In the sunlight, in the pain

Everyone I've ever known needs a friend
A warm hand in a hand
Every woman and man

You want to make a good friend, do it now
Brother why wait around?
Sister don't let me down
Cause you pass right by a friend
And they might never come again.

Don't you know me?
What I really mean
Is there something here that you can understand?
I am not afraid to open up my hand
And I stretch it out to see
If it's taken by a friend.

Lyrics and music by Michael Tomlinson
Seattle, Washington, 1985

ENDNOTES

Chapter One:

1. M.J. Ryan, *The Fabric of the Future* (Berkeley, CA: Conari Press, 1998), 13.

2. Positive and negative aspects taken from José Stevens, Ph.D., and Simon Warwick-Smith, *The Michael Handbook* (Sonoma, CA: Warwick Press, 1990), 104-105.

3. Emily Baumbach, *Celebrities: The Complete Michael Database, Personality Profiles for Over 1,000 Famous People* (San Rafael, CA: Causalworks, 1996), 13-51.

4. Interview with Emily Baumbach (May 24, 2001).

5. Stevens and Warwick-Smith, *The Michael Handbook*, 107.

6. Baumbach, *Celebrities: The Complete Michael Database, Personality Profiles for Over 1,000 Famous People*, 13-51.

7. Interview with Emily Baumbach (May 24, 2001).

8. Ibid.

9. Baumbach, *Celebrities: The Complete Michael Database, Personality Profiles for Over 1,000 Famous People*, 13-51.

10. Interview with Emily Baumbach (May 24, 2001).

11. Baumbach, *Celebrities: The Complete Michael Database, Personality Profiles for Over 1,000 Famous People*, 13-51.

12. Stevens and Warwick-Smith, *The Michael Handbook*, 87.

13. Baumbach, *Celebrities: The Complete Michael Database, Personality Profiles for Over 1,000 Famous People*, 13-51.

14. Ibid.

15. Interview with Emily Baumbach (May 24, 2001).

16. Baumbach, *Celebrities: The Complete Michael Database, Personality Profiles for Over 1,000 Famous People*, 13-51.

Chapter Two:

1. Robert E. (Dusty) Staub II, *The Heart of Leadership: 12 Practices of Courageous Leaders* (Provo, UT: Executive Excellence Publishing, 2000), 65.

Chapter Three:

1. Judith Graham, ed., *Current Biography Yearbook* (New York: The Wilson Company, 1992), 479.

2. Ibid., 482.

3. Open Keynote Address by Aung San Suu Kyi to the NGO Forum on Women in Beijing, 1995. http://www.ibiblio.org/freebuma/assk/assk3-2a.html.

4. Michele Manceaux, "Fearless Aung San Suu Kyi," *Marie Claire Magazine* (May 1996, Singapore edition), 36.

5. José Stevens and Simon Warwick-Smith, *The Michael Handbook* (Sonoma, CA: Warwick Press, 1990), 191.

6. Ibid.

7. Emily Baumbach, *Celebrities: The Complete Michael Database, Personality Profiles for Over 1,000 Famous People* (San Rafael, CA: Causalworks, 1996), 7-51.

8. Ibid.

9. Ibid.

10. Ibid.

11. Ibid.

12. Ibid.

13. Ibid.

14. Stevens and Warwick-Smith, *The Michael Handbook*, 140-141.

15. Robert E. Staub II, *The Seven Acts of Courage* (Provo, UT: Executive Excellence Publishing, 1999), 17.

16. Ibid., 58-63.
17. Ibid., 66.
18. Ibid., 101.
19. Ibid., 105.
20. Ibid., 106.
21. Ibid., 115.
22. Ibid., 67-68.

Chapter Four:

1. José Stevens and Simon Warwick-Smith, *The Michael Handbook* (Sonoma, CA: Warwick Press, 1990), 125.
2. Ibid., 191.
3. Ibid., 195.
4. Emily Baumbach, *Celebrities: The Complete Michael Database, Personality Profiles for Over 1,000 Famous People* (San Rafael, CA: Causalworks, 1996), 9-10, 13-51.
5. Ibid.
6. Ibid.
7. Ibid.
8. Ibid.
9. Ibid.
10. Ibid.

Chapter Six:

1. John W. Travis, M.D. and Regina Sara Ryan, *Wellness Workbook* (Berkeley, CA: Ten Speed Press, 1988), 169.
2. Jack Canfield, Mark Victor Hansen, Jennifer Read Hawthorne and Marci Shimoff, *Chicken Soup for the Woman's Soul* (Deerfield Beach, FL: Health Communications, Inc., 1996), 78-80.
3. Meyer Friedman and Diane Ulmer, *Treating Type A Behavior and Your Heart* (New York: Knopf, 1984), 83-102.
4. S. Haynes, et al. *American Journal of Epidemiology III*, 1980, 37-58.

5. Michael Castleman, "Are You a Type A Woman?" *Medical Self-Care*, Inverness, CA., 1985, 32.

6. Friedman and Ulmer, *Treating Type A Behavior and Your Heart*, 83-102.

7. Ibid., 83-102.

8. Ibid.

9. Travis and Ryan, *Wellness Workbook*, 64.

10. Frances Sheridan Goulart, "Are You Your Own Best Friend?" *Changes*, March-April, 1990, 34-38.

11. Karen Turner, "Building the Sacred Vessel of Relationship," *Yoga Journal*, May-June 1987, 35.

12. Breath Exercise, Travis and Ryan, *Wellness Workbook*, 27.

13. Breath Exercise, Travis and Ryan, *Wellness Workbook*, 34.

14. Caroline Myss, *Why People Don't Heal and How They Can* (New York: Harmony Books, 1997), 113.

15. Daniel Goleman, Ph.D., and Tara Bennett-Goleman, "Moving Toward Mindfulness," *American Health*, 1987, 82.

16. Valerie Andrews, "Rekindling a Sense of Place," *Common Boundary*, November/December, 1990, 24.

17. Ibid., 27.

18. Frances Nixon, *Mysteries of Memory Unfold* (Chemanius, BC, Canada: Magnetic Publishers), 1977.

19. Carl Jung, *Civilization in Transition*. Vol. 10 of *The Collected Works of Carl Jung* (New York: Pantheon, Bollingen Series 20, 1964), 49.

20. Virginia Williams, Ph.D., and Redford Williams, M.D., *Lifeskills: 8 Simple Ways to Build Stronger Relationships, Communicate More Clearly, Improve Your Health* (Times Books, Random House, 1997), 241.

BIBLIOGRAPHY

Adler, Gerhard, and Aniela Jaffé, eds. Letter to M.R. Brabad-Iasaac, 22.7-39. *C. G. Jung*, vol. 1: 274-5.

Andrews, Valerie. "Rekindling a Sense of Place." *Common Boundary* (November/December 1990).

Angelou, Maya. *Wouldn't Take Nothing For My Journey Now*. New York: Bantam Books.

Arnot, Bob. *The Biology of Success*. New York: Little, Brown and Company, 2000.

Bach, Richard. *Illusions: The Adventures of a Reluctant Messiah*. New York: Dell Publishing.

Baumbach, Emily. *Celebrities: The Complete Michael Database, Personality Profiles for Over 1,000 Famous People*. San Rafael, CA: Causalworks, 1996.

Bolen, Jean Shinoda, M.D. *Goddesses in Everywoman: A New Psychology of Women*. San Francisco: Harper & Row, 1984.

Briles, Judith, Dr. *Woman to Woman 2000: Becoming Sabotage Savvy in the New Millennium*. Far Hills, NJ: New Horizon Press, 1999.

Campbell, Joseph. *The Masks of God: Creative Mythology*. New York: The Viking Press,   1968.

Canfield, Jack, and Mark Victor Hansen, Jennifer Read Hawthorne, and Marci Shimoff. *Chicken Soup for the Woman's Soul*. Deerfield Beach, FL: Health Communications, 1996.

Capra, Fritjof. *The Turning Point.* London: Fontana Paperback, Collins Publishing Group, 1982.

Carr-Ruffino, Norma, Ph.D. *The Promotable Woman: 10 Essential Skills for the New Millennium.* Franklin Lakes, NJ: Career Press, 1997.

Castleman, Michael. "Are You a Type A Woman?" *Medical Self-Care.* Inverness, CA.

Celebrating Women. Edina, MN: Heartland Sampler, Inc, 1992.

Christ, Carol. *Laughter of Aphrodite: Reflections on a Journey to the Goddess.* San Francisco: Harper & Row, 1987.

Dass, Ram with Stephen Levine. *Grist For the Mill.* Berkeley, CA: Celestial Arts, 1987.

Denfeld, Rene. *The New Victorians: A Young Woman's Challenge to the Old Feminist Order.* New York: Warner Books, 1995.

Dyer, Wayne. *Wisdom of the Ages: A Modern Master Brings Eternal Truth into Everyday Life.* New York: HarperCollins, 1998.

Fox, Matthew. *Original Blessing: A Primer in Creation Spirituality.* Sante Fe, NM: Bear & Company, 1983.

Friedman, Meyer, and Diane Ulmer. *Type A Behavior and Your Health.* New York: Knopf, 1984.

Gadon, Elinor W. *The Once & Future Goddess.* San Francisco: Harper & Row, 1989.

Gates, Doris. *Athena: The Warrior Goddess.* New York: The Viking Press, 1972.

Gawain, Shakti with Laurel King. *Living In the Light: A Guide to Personal and Planetary Transformation.* San Rafael, CA: New World Library, 1986.

Goldberg, Natalie. *Writing Down the Bones.* Boston, MA: Shambala Publications, 1986.

Goleman, Daniel, Ph.D., and Tara Bennett-Goleman. "Moving Toward Mindfulness." *American Health* (1987).

Goulart, Frances Sheridan. "Are You Your Own Best Friend?" *Changes* (March-April 1990).

Bibliography

Graham, Judith, ed. *Current Biography Yearbook.* New York: The Wilson Company, 1992.

Griscom, Chris. *Ecstasy Is a New Frequency.* Sante Fe, NM: Bear and Company, 1987.

Griscom, Chris. *The Healing of Emotion: Awakening the Fearless Self.* New York: Simon & Schuster, 1988.

Harris, Maxine. *Down from the Pedestal: Moving Beyond Idealized Images of Womanhood.* New York: Doubleday, 1994.

Hay, Louise. *You Can Heal Your Life.* Santa Monica, CA: Hay House, 1984.

Haynes, S. et al. *Journal of Epidemiology III.* 1980.

Jung, Carl. *Civilization in Transition, Vol. 10 of The Collected Works of Carl Jung.* New York: Pantheon Bollingen Series 20, 1964.

Johnson, Caesar. *To See a World in a Grain of Sand.* Norwalk, CT: C.R. Gibson Company.

Keay, Kathy. *Laughter, Silence and Shouting: An Anthology of Women's Prayers.* London: HarperCollins UK, 1994.

Keirsey, David, and Marilyn Bates. *Please Understand Me: Character & Temperament Types.* Gnosology Book Ltd., 1984.

Keyes, Ken. *Handbook to Higher Consciousness.* Coos Bay, OR: Living Love Center, 1975.

Kyi, Aung San Suu. Open Keynote Address to the NGO Forum on Women in Beijing. 1995. http://www.ibiblio.org/freebuma/assk/assk3-2a.html.

Levine, Stephen. *Who Dies? An Investigation of Conscious Living and Conscious Dying.* New York: Anchor Press/Doubleday, 1982.

Maher, John M., and Dennie Briggs. *An Open Life: Joseph Campbell in Conversation with Michael Toms.* Burdett, NY: Larsen Publications, 1988.

Manceaux, Michele. "Fearless Aung San Suu Kyi." *Marie Claire Magazine* (May 1996, Singapore edition).

Martin, Katherine. *Women of Courage: Inspiring Stories from the Women Who Lived Them.* Novato, CA: New World Library, 1999.

Myss, Caroline, Ph.D., *Why People Don't Heal and How They Can.* New York: Harmony Books, 1997.

Nixon, Frances. *Mysteries of Memory Unfold.* Chemanius, BC, Canada: Magnetic Publishers, 1977.

Osborne, Mary Pope. *Favorite Greek Myths.* New York: Scholastic, 1989.

Rappaport, Doreen. *American Women: Their Lives in Their Words.* New York: Thomas U. Crowell, 1990.

Ross, John Munder, Ph.D. *The Male Paradox.* New York: Simon & Schuster, 1992.

Ryan, M.J. *The Fabric of the Future.* Berkeley, CA: Conari Press, 1998.

Ryan, Regina Sara. *The Woman Awake: Feminine Wisdom for Spiritual Life.* Prescott, AZ: Holm Press, 1998.

Sark. *Succulent Wild Woman: Dancing With Your Wonder Full Self.* New York: Fireside Book, 1997.

Satir, Virginia. *Meditations & Inspirations.* Berkeley, CA: Celestial Arts, 1985.

Shinn, Florence Scovel. *The Game of Life.* Marina del Rey, CA: DeVorss & Company, 1925.

Starhawk. *The Spiral Dance: A Rebirth of the Ancient Religion of the Great Goddess.* San Francisco: Harper & Row, 1979.

Staub, Robert E. (Dusty), II. *The Heart of Leadership: 12 Practices of Courageous Leaders.* Provo, UT: Executive Excellence Publishing, 2000.

Staub, Robert E. (Dusty), II. *The Seven Acts of Courage.* Provo, UT: Executive Excellence Publishing, 1999.

Stevens, José, Ph.D., and Simon Warwick-Smith. *The Michael Handbook.* Sonoma, CA: Warwick Press, 1990.

Stevens, José, Ph.D. *Transforming Your Dragons: How to Turn Fear Patterns into Personal Power.* Sante Fe, NM: Bear & Company, 1994.

Swan, James A. *Sacred Places: How the Living Earth Seeks Our Friendship*. Sante Fe, NM: Bear & Company, 1990.

Travis, John W., M.D., and Regina Sara Ryan. *Wellness Workbook: Second Edition*. Berkeley, CA: Ten Speed Press, 1988.

Turner, Karen. "Building the Sacred Vessel of Relationship." *Yoga Journal* (March-June 1987).

Usher, Kerry. *Heroes, Gods & Emperors from Roman Mythology*. New York: Schocken Books, 1983.

Vanzant, Iyanla. *One Day My Soul Just Opened Up: 40 Days and 40 Nights Towards Spiritual Strength and Personal Growth*. New York: Fireside, 1998.

Vaughn, Frances E. *Awakening Intuition*. Garden City, NJ: Anchor Press/Doubleday, 1979.

Walsch, Neale Donald. *Conversations with God: book 3*. Charlottesville, VA: Hampton Roads Publishing, 1998.

Whitmont, Edward C. *Return of the Goddess*. New York: Crossroads, 1982.

Williams, Virginia, Ph.D., and Redford Williams, M.D. *Lifeskills: 8 Simple Ways to Build Stronger Relationships, Communicate More Clearly and Improve Your Health*. Times Books/Random House, 1997.

Williamson, Marianne. *A Woman's Worth*. New York: Ballantine Books, 1993.

Wolf, Naomi. *Fire With Fire: The New Female Power and How it Will Change the 21st Century*. New York: Random House, 1993.

Woodman, Marion. *Addiction to Perfection: The Still Unravished Bride*. Toronto, Canada: Inner City Books, 1982.

Yogananda, Paramahansa. *Autobiography of a Yogi*. San Rafael, CA: Self-Realization Fellowship, 1974.

Yogananda, Paramahansa. *Scientific Healing Affirmations*. San Rafael, CA: Self-Realization Fellowship, 1981.

PERMISSIONS

Excerpts from: *The Michael Handbook* by José Stevens and Simon Warwick-Smith, Sonoma, CA: Warwick Press, 1990.

Excerpts from: *Celebrities: The Complete Michael Database, Personality Profiles for Over 1,000 Famous People* by Emily Baumbach, San Rafael, CA: Causalworks, 1996.

Selected song lyrics from: "Living Things," *Living Things CD* by Michael Tomlinson, Canadian Train Music, Mesa Records, 1991., http://www.michaeltomlinson.com.

Selected poems from: *Laughter, Silence and Shouting: An Anthology of Women's Prayers* by Kathy Keay, London: Harper Collins UK, 1994.

Excerpts from: *The Heart of Leadership: 12 Practices of Courageous Leaders* by Robert E. Staub II, Provo, UT: Executive Excellence Publishing, 2000.

Song lyrics from: "The Way We're Going," *Face Up In The Rain CD* by Michael Tomlinson, 1989. http://www.michaeltomlinson.com.

Excerpts and selected quotes from: *Women of Courage: Inspiring Stories from the Women Who Lived Them* by Katherine Martin, Novato, CA: New World Library, 1999.

Excerpts from: *The Seven Acts of Courage* by Robert E. Staub II, Provo, UT: Executive Excellence Publishing, 1999.

BC Comic by permission of Johnny Hart and Creators Syndicate, Inc., dated December 11, 1992, 5777 W. Century Blvd., Suite 700, Los Angeles, CA, 90045.

Excerpts from: *The Wellness Workbook: Second Edition* by Dr. John Travis and Regina Sara Ryan, Berkeley, CA: Bear & Company, 1988.

Poem, "Angela's Word," by Barbara Bassett, originally published in *Chicken Soup for the Woman's Soul*, edited by Jack Canfield, Mark Victor Hansen, Jennifer Read Hawthorne, and Marci Shimoff, Deerfield Beach, FL: Health Communications, 1996.

Excerpts reprinted from: "Are You a Type-A Woman?" by Michael Castleman, originally published in *Medical Self-Care Magazine*, Inverness, CA: 1985.

Poem, "Praise to the Women on My Journey," reprinted with permission from the Reverend Melissa Bowers, originally published in *Chicken Soup for the Woman's Soul*, edited by Jack Canfield, Mark Victor Hansen, Jennifer Read Hawthorne, and Marci Shimoff, Deerfield Beach, FL: Health Communications, 1996.

Song lyrics from: "By A Friend," written by Michael Tomlinson from the *Still Believe CD*, Desert Rain Records, Seattle Washington, 1988. http://www.michaeltomlinson.com.

INDEX

COMMON BOUNDARIES

Common Boundaries is a leadership consulting and communications company that evolved from the strategic vision of founder Debra J. Gawrych. From childhood, she had the dream of teaching and guiding others to fulfill their dreams.

The company is dedicated to helping others realize their visions and facilitate improved communications. This is achieved through:

➤ Custom-designed programs for businesses and organizations

➤ Programs tailored for universities and schools

➤ Keynote speeches

➤ Books, multimedia presentations, and articles

➤ Personal coaching

Common Boundaries also has a charter to give back to the community and has made a commitment to give a portion of the proceeds to Breast Cancer Research and the Women's World Banking Organization. A portion of the proceeds from the sale of every book goes to Breast Cancer Research: Friends You Can Count On, Expedition Inspiration, and the Susan G. Komen Foundation (Race For the Cure) as well as the Women's World Banking Organization. See the back of the book for more details.

Learn more about this dynamic company at:
www.commonboundaries.com

Or contact us at:
**Common Boundaries
P.O. Box 39445
Greensboro, NC 27438
336-288-8554**

Praise for Common Boundaries Consulting and Communications Programs and Keynotes

"You have inspired many students and offered advice that has enabled them to further develop their leadership style. In working with you on a number of projects what shines through is your ability to connect with a variety of individuals and engage an audience so that they get the most out of the experience. It is a pleasure working with you, and I look forward to our partnership in taking the Buck Rodgers Business Leadership Program to new heights. You truly are a visionary."

— Kris Reid, Buck Rodgers Business Leadership Program,
Miami University

"I can't imagine a stronger kick-off for our Mom's Empowerment Series than your workshop on the aspects of sisterhood and the different roles women play today. Your willingness to share specifics about your own life, home, and career speaks to the earnestness with which you approach your work."

— Dena Harris, Women's Resource Center

"The program was a dynamic introduction to models of leadership, using a variety of approaches—personal stories of Debra Gawrych and her team, small group discussions, connections to images of women in the media, and references to archetypal models. This combination of subject and strategies pushed students to think about themselves as leaders and to question common assumptions."

— Margaret Grissom, Assistant Headmaster,
and Theo Coonrod, Headmaster, St. Mary's School

"Your presentation [at the Women In Cable & Telecommunications of the Carolinas program] was of the highest quality and included truly valuable information for our membership."

— Andi Desautels, Time Warner Cable

"You have an important message to deliver, and I have received many positive comments from the students regarding your presentation."

— Jill Sparks, Appalachian State University

"I enjoyed your presentation very much. You do a great job. I'm guessing that you already have another project under way."

— Terrence McConnell, Professor

More from Debra Gawrych: Gutsy Girls

Look for the first book of the Gutsy Girls series—*Gutsy Girls Climb*—in the fall of 2003. This fiction series for girls in middle school and early grades of high school focuses on empowering girls through sports. Entertaining storylines teach how to resolve conflict through cooperation rather than by working against each other.

Following the principles of Common Boundaries, a portion of the proceeds from the sale of each book goes to the governing organization that supports girls in that sport.

Community Involvement

Friends…You Can Count On is the nation's only nonprofit organization solely dedicated to finding methods of detecting breast cancer earlier. Founder Martha Kaley was inspired by her personal experience with a cancerous tumor that went undetected even after a mammogram. Instead of feeling like a victim, she decided to form an organization that would focus on this neglected area of research.

Common Boundaries is proud to support the efforts of this amazing organization and welcomes you to join with us to see the day when breast cancer research is no longer needed.

For more information about Friends…You Can Count On:
1-888-792-3062 or www.earlier.org.

ORDER FORM

The Seven Aspects of Sisterhood: Empowering Women Through Self-Discovery

Name _____

Address _____

City _____

State _____ Zip _____

Phone _____ Fax _____

E-mail _____

Number of copies @ $23.95 each _____

Subtotal _____

NC residents add 6.5% tax _____

Shipping and handling _____

Total _____

Shipping and handling: 1–2 books, $4.00; 3–6 books, $6.00; 6–10 books, $8.00.
For overnight and international shipping, call 336-288-8554 for rates.

Payment

❏ Check _____ ❏ Credit Card / ❏ Visa ❏ MasterCard

Card Number _____

Expiration date _____

Name on Card _____

Signature _____

Mail form and payment to:

Common Boundaries, P.O. Box 39445, Greensboro, NC 27438

Order online:

Order books at our convenient Web site: www.commonboundaries.com

Interested in Common Boundaries programs?

_____

_____

_____

_____

Thanks for your support
www.commonboundaries.com